Memoirs of a Migrant Child

Emma González

Aknowledgements

I dedicate this book first and foremost, to the **Blessed Mother Teresa**, who was my inspiration. Her unyielding spirit guided me to write this memoir. Thank you **God**, for allowing me to channel her and enlighten me along this awe-inspiring pilgrimage of soul searching and healing.

To **Arnulfo (Arnie)**, my wonderful husband who embraced my experiences as a migrant child and who encouraged me to write them.

To **Andy (Melinda), Lisa (Orlie)**, my children, and grandchildren, **Emma, Raul, Adam**, and **Avalise**, all of you were ultimately the light of those iridescent - hued horizons I loved as a child. To my mother, **Maria Isabel Ornelas González**, my half-brother, **Eladio (Laco) Torres**.

To my lifelong friends: **Patty Schneider Truesdell, Jody Lauer Jimenez, Raymond Schneider** and many others, whose friendships I took to heart through years, culminating in our recent reunion. After reconnecting fifty years later, I recognize how valuable a treasure our bond remains and feel a deep gratitude to you and the caring people in Ovid, Colorado so many years ago. Their acceptance of the little migrant girl into their homes and heart gave me courage and confidence to persevere in my dreams.

A special "Thank You" to those who gave me my educational opportunities -- **Mr. Tom Kobayashi** and my elementary teachers **Mrs. Melba Snyder** and **Mrs. Joan Brownell,** who never stopped encouraging me. Because of you, Ovid will always be my hometown.

A special recognition to **Alvaro Rodriguez,** who advised me to write "from the heart."

Finally, to **Charlene Kuprel**, who helped me with editing and ideas, and who became a true friend along our writing journey. Your words of encouragement and prayers were heartfelt.

PREFACE

For months the voice echoed in my head. I tried to ignore it. But, day and night it repeated the same message: "Emma, it's your time, now."

What did it mean? Why was it pursuing me? "My time" for what? Life threw me a hell of a curve when I was unexpectedly laid off from my job of eleven years with the County's Victims' Services Department in the District Attorney's Office. I was fifty-nine. Funding for my position came from grants and because of a technical glitch, our grant was denied. Furthermore, my employer did not make the effort to find other sources of funding.

Why did this happen to me? I knew these victims' pain. Victimization had struck my family long before I held that position. I lost a half-sister to a drunk driver and two nephews were murdered in separate incidents. Finally, I had found the most rewarding job, a "calling," so to speak. I assisted victims of crime, all ages, from counseling referrals, assistance for medical, and burials for homicide victims. To me, the most heart wrenching cases involved murdered and sexually abused children. Did my years of service to the county count for anything? I hope it did for the thousands of victims I helped. To this date, I am thankful I was there for them. Why was I taken away from what I thought was my purpose?

It was difficult to see my way clearly afterwards. I had many questions. I was two years shy of completing twenty years of service to Hidalgo County. I felt betrayed and hurt. Then, I found out more people were hired as I was being let go. Enraged, I wanted to lash out. I was fuming - my pulse racing, but at that very moment something held me back. Reluctantly, I held my tongue. Perhaps it was Divine intervention comforting me, I glanced directly at Blessed Mother Teresa's portrait hanging on my office wall. I wondered what she would do in my situation. She had been my friend and co-worker for years and I refused to disrespect her in that manner. She looked pensive, deep in thought, one with God. Gradually, I let go of the poison brewing in me. I calmed down and asked for forgiveness. It was not worth getting into a confrontational blowout with the outcome turning out worse than my reaction to the pink-slip notice.

For the next three months, I grieved for the current and future victims and myself. At the end of each day, I'd cross out that day on my wall calendar. Gradually, I began to take items from the credenza in my office. Some included small gifts from the many victims I had helped, my grandkids' pictures, and my personal belongings. I was in tears as I loaded the items into the car. The only thing that remained at the end was Mother Teresa's portrait.

How Mother Teresa Came to Me

Several years earlier, David Reyes, an assistant prosecutor and a member of Saint Joseph Catholic Church in Edinburg asked me if I would buy some raffle tickets for their fundraiser. I bought the last two tickets he had. I didn't mind contributing to that church, both my kids had attended their school for more than fifteen years. I gladly paid him the one-hundred dollars.

Weeks went by and I forgot about them. One Monday morning, David came into my office to advise me that I had won a prize. I wanted to win the Toyota Camry, the grand prize! I envisioned the keys handed to me. Instead, I was presented with a brown folded cardboard. I unfolded it to reveal a black and white portrait of Mother Teresa. "Holy Cow! Is this my prize?" I asked. I paid one hundred dollars to get a picture of Mother Teresa? A white envelope slid off her portrait containing a letter from the Franciscan Brother who photographed and interviewed her in Detroit, just prior to her death. In his letter, he wrote how he was selected to interview her and the discourse between them. A chill went through me. I shook as I read it. David was elated! He told me the photographer was his sibling, Brother Vincent Reyes, Member of the Capuchin Franciscan Order. Brother Vincent had donated his only two personal copies of her portrait to the church to be raffled. What are the odds of me winning a prize? Even more, what were the odds of winning *her* portrait? Thousands of raffle tickets were sold; however, she selected who would be the ultimate person to receive her. Call it a pre-destined celestial bequest. A sign I would not ignore. The Camry would have lost its value the minute I drove it off the lot. However, *SHE* was priceless! I felt privileged. She came to help me help others. Her life's work had been helping the needy, a dedication we shared.

Her portrait hung in my office for years until November 30, 2011, at five p.m. when she and I walked out of the courthouse building. She still resides contentedly in my home. She would soon give me a new direction for my life.

Dreams Have a Purpose

I've always believed that as one door closes on you, God, in his infinite universe, opens others. I trust Him whole heartedly to lead me as His Will chose. His signs were my guides as in the story of Mother Teresa's portrait. Once more, at a critical time, something mystical and divine would intervene in my life.

About nine months earlier before being "canned," I had a dream as vivid and real as were the characters, the time and places. This dream came to me very intensely and was so memorable in form: the colors, the shapes, the people, even the smells, heightened my profound communication with the apparition. My story to be written was revealed to me in complete detail: even to the minutia of the artwork of the book cover, that was undeniably perfect, depicting etched memories of a poignant time in my early life.

A distinctive, melodic angelic voice, echoed, "Emma, it's your time now."
The charismatic voice continued to call to me. I remember its form materializing, like waves of a mirage on a desert. This heavenly being had a crown of soft blue halos that glowed above its head and then encompassed the rest of its essence. It radiated a warmth and a nurturing comfort, from this arose a euphoria I had never felt before. Throughout the entire dream, we "conversed." Not audibly, but somehow I understood the "being's" urgent message.

In my dream, we ascended above the clouds, to a pitch-black sky, suddenly star-lit with cosmic twinkling stars, a shimmer-like mist blanketed me, and a silvery sheen glowed about me. I was airborne, gently gliding over open fields descending ethereally: the panorama of my life as a child. I saw glimpses of myself in places where I lived from about the age of five until the age of fifteen. I relived my early years with incredible detail, sequence of events and places I visited. I was told to write about that period of my life.

"I remember. I remember," I whispered as I awoke, sobbing.

My understanding of this Divine request came later. I would understand in due time the reasons behind this request, and the fragments that would fit together like pieces of a puzzle. I knew then, that higher forces were involved. Another path had opened for me to follow. I would write.

One day as we rode in our Navigator, we had our grandchildren with us, Emma and Raulito. The CDs in our car consisted of "oldies," songs from my era, the late fifties and sixties reminding me of my past. Just as we pulled up to the window teller of the bank, my all-time favorite song by Frankie Lymon began to play, "Little Bitty Pretty One." The unique beat and rhythm set the mood, for finger – snapping and humming.

My two-year-old grandson began to bob his head to the beat as he sat strapped in his car seat. He had put on his "shades" which we had left right next to him in the middle console. He looked so cool! Arnie, my husband, nudged me and whispered "look at him!" As I turned to see him, he was into the song, as if he had heard it other times. I snapped my fingers and he caught on and then, Emma, my granddaughter joined us. About the third or fourth snap, I "snapped" too!

"THAT'S IT !!!," I yelled out. "That's it, that's it," I kept repeating. I wasn't referring to Raulito snapping to the beat. Right then and there in a sudden flashback, I instantly became clear aware of the chore the voice had given me eight months earlier. For one, it had warned me I would be laid off from my job. But, it had also commanded me to write about the time I was a migrant kid in the fifties and sixties! I now knew what this voice wanted of me! "I am supposed to write about those years," I screamed out to Arnie. "That's what "it" has been telling me to do!" I couldn't contain myself with the realization I had such a request from a spiritual source. It had been so insistent, even literally stopping me in my tracks fracturing my foot, just out of nowhere to push me. I felt the pain shoot up to my head, and even then, I denied that it had anything to do with the revelation. Surely, this mystical, angelic image was unyielding, determined to get my attention. Ultimately, I did take this sign seriously. The accident "knocked" some sense into my willful head. Now, I would begin searching for what I was to do.

For the next three months, I was incapacitated as I tried to heal. I spent time sorting things out. The main thing I focused on was the continuous "calling" to tell my story. Finally, I resigned to what was imminent, an awareness of spiritual direction had touched me. I realized I was chosen for a reason. A brilliant light brushed by me. The three-month dark period of my life became illuminated. I was to share my childhood's life experiences.

In all the commotion and my yelling out the revelation, we forgot the bank teller was trying to talk to us. Our windows remained rolled up, and I was holding the deposit slip, waving it in the air, in a totally - gone - nuts moment! Once more, I glanced at my grandkids sitting behind us. A child led me to "see" what I hadn't been capable of seeing. I calmed down enough to give the deposit to Arnie to hand to the bank teller, she looked positively peeved at us, rather at the behavior of two mature adults, one of them having a mystic fulfillment, long overdue.

Although I had written articles and stories for my high school's literary magazine and newspaper several "centuries" ago, I never imagined writing a book, my memoirs, at this age. I had no intention whatsoever to "write" anything. How would I begin?

Consciously, I sensed a "presence" guiding me. Once I began to write my memoirs, they flowed out so rapidly that I had to keep a hand-held tape recorder by my bed at night, and hung another one around my neck during the day to record bits and pieces of memories, deeply and reclusively imbedded in my mind. I never knew when I'd be "inspired" by a story, immediately record it, so as to not forget what had flashed before me. I was amazed at the details so vividly etched in my mind and the facts I could recall with incredible details, specifically of events that occurred more than fifty years ago.

The memories poured into my mind, flooding me with images I had not thought about in decades! Vivid pictures and thoughts streamed in as in a raging flood. I awoke in the middle of the night or right at dawn, exhausted, after recalling a monsoon of different experiences I had lived during those ten years I was a migrant until

I was fifteen. Arnie awoke startled only to find me looking dazed, as in a dream. I'd utter to him, "she was with me, again." He would try to calm me down – he knew I was "re-living" another episode. There were times I broke down in exasperation in broad daylight and at night, screaming aloud, uncontrollably. I could not grasp the magnitude of this experience, and I'd cry to let out the frustration, the unintelligibility of this Divine request. Even more so, I avoided public places, for fear of breaking down, if a sad thought suddenly pinned me for an outburst of tears.

I seemed lost in a sea of distressing memories, each one submerging me to a depth of no return. I felt my soul ache, my spirit dimmed to any light I sought. All this is for what, I questioned myself. "Why am I putting myself though this? Why me? More importantly, why now? What would I accomplish carrying out this spirit's wish?" I was more desperate than ever. I turned to constant prayer and meditation for relief and for answers. I waited for responses. Finally, He would answer. God's grace touched my soul; renewed it in His love and I surrendered to His Holy guidance. His remarkable gift of love deepened my determination to continue. Without a doubt, I knew what God's plan was for me. He unshackled these stories and brought them to surface – to my conscious mind, and He wants me to write them. It became evident that nothing could stop me from writing.

Surely, I would not be the same person who had fought Blessed Mother Teresa's message. It *is* she. The angelic apparition of Blessed Mother Teresa would enlighten me to "re-live" my life's story as a child. Each time she appeared to me subconsciously and in my dream, her facial profile became more defined. She, too, has an interest, so to speak. Somehow, I sensed what it may come to be, but for now, she _is_ my inspiration and her motivational spirit accompanies me. As I wrote each memoir, her saintly, raspy voice echoed, "Emma, it's your time, now." I felt it exceedingly compelling in my heart to write these memoirs; given the devoted and indomitable strength of her spirit – I placed my trust in her – and in God's Will. Within their perpetual trust, I let go and I began to write.

TABLE OF CONTENTS

The Labor Begins

Still pitch dark, the peacefulness of the morning was shattered by the sound of a truck's misfiring engine, as it pulled up to our house to take us to the field. Half-asleep and wrapped in blankets, I was placed in the back of the truck with my half-brothers, parents, and half- sister. Getting to the field didn't take long. This change was a strange experience for this five year old.

Soon after, I watched my family ready themselves to take to the field. The foreman who transported us from Texas, handed each of them hoes. Still wrapped in blankets I was left on the ground. As I realized what was happening before my eyes, I began screaming, at the top of my lungs, begging them not to leave. "No te vayas, Mommy," ("Don't go Mommy!") I cried hysterically, over and over. Mom assured me that she would be back. Nevertheless, the coldness in her voice did not convince me she told the truth. "Quédate, y regreso al rato" ("Stay, I'll be back shortly"), she shouted sternly. My family members each told me, "Quédate allí!" ("Stay there!") My chest pounded with sheer fear and disbelief, I beseeched them, pleaded for them to come back. Before this moment, I had never felt abandoned. How could they leave me?

My sobbing destroyed the tranquility of that morning and the many mornings that followed. Numbness crept over me. Thinking back, I don't know if that was because of the cold, the shock, fear, disbelief, or all of them combined. Each second they walked further and further away from me the more the pain grew, joined by hopeless resignation as the family each took to the rows of beets, hoeing.

I had no place to stay except in the irrigation ditch, safeguarding our food and water containers. Each second I was alone, I watched my family, but they disappeared into the distance. I wailed, "Where are you?" When they vanished I didn't know if they reached the other end of the field or simply left me forever. I climbed back down into the ditch and covered myself. In there, no one heard the whimpering of a desperate, abandoned child whose strained and exhausted voice faded to a moan. Time stopped. Over and over, I'd tell myself "they will come back soon, they will come back soon." And, they eventually did, after an eternity they returned for water, food, and simply to regain energy.

Each time they took to the rows, I'd burst out uncontrollably. But, I went unnoticed, agitated, and got no assurance I'd be all right. I tried running after them, but got verbally warned without a doubt I'd be physically dealt with if I didn't return to the ditch. I remember. I remember. That agony and torture tore my soul. I was alone.

When dusk set in, the foreman came to take us home. That first day was long. Still numb from the day's trauma, everything felt so surreal. I felt misplaced from reality. The morning began with abandonment by my own family, by the days end it seemed I was not even part of them anymore. All was beyond the comprehension of a five-year-old. I just understood the desertion without an explanation. What had I done to them that merited this cruel punishment?

Fear, disbelief, and feeling unwanted became an ongoing nightmare. Day in and day out, they remained uncaring, cold-hearted, negligent and outright mean to me. They took to the fields like zombies staggering through the rows. In my eyes, the horizon swallowed them up until they re-appeared out of thin air when they reached the edge. The distance between me and my family was a million miles or more, as they walked acre after acre. But, Dad declared they only went half a mile or more each way, times a million rows!

When they returned they appeared dazed, almost comatose. I noticed the adoption of a slave mind set, and witnessed misery in their eyes and an overall physical change. They appeared as if lost and saddened. What I couldn't comprehend was their unsettling behavior. Too often this abrupt behavior frightened me, and I wondered if something terrible had happened to them during the time they disappeared at the other end of the field, or worse yet, I worried I had done something terribly wrong to upset them.

Over time, I would understand. All the while, they were burdened with their need to survive the inescapably arduous fate of field labor. In my isolation from them, I grieved. While, we appeared a picture perfect family, they were miserable, as isolated in their own world, as I was in mine.

The sugar beet growing season reached full force. The first phase of the season was planting the beets, if they had not already been in the ground. By the time we got there, most farmers had done their part. Their "hands" pulled the weeds at the first sight of sprouting beet plants all along the entire row, and at the same time they thinned the plants 6-8 inches apart to provide space for growth. I listened to conversations between the boys and Dad. They claimed it would be a long season before the beet's harvest. I had understood we'd be there for just a few days.

Four a.m. came too soon. It felt I slept just a few minutes since we went to bed at night, then I was awakened in the middle of my REM sleep. The start of another day was a typical morning without the actual daylight. I was too confused to even ask why we were going to work in the middle of the night. At Dad's firm command, everybody else hurried out of bed and were dressed in seconds.

Meanwhile, the aroma of freshly brewed coffee travelled into the room where I slept. This scent was my alarm before being abruptly pulled out of bed. Mom got up much earlier than the rest of us to prepare the day's breakfast and lunch. The first thing she put on the stove was a pot of coffee. The pot was an old fashion metal pot that brewed coffee granules in a perforated metal strainer inside the pot. The percolating sound alerted me to be ready.

Simultaneously, she prepared breakfast. That wood burning stove met its match when Mom lit all the burners. The glowing fire devoured the crackling firewood as she cooked. The burning wood added a unique smoke flavoring to all the cooking, while the scent of fried onions, bacon and eggs, and seasoned potatoes cooked in huge iron skillets enveloped the house. It sparked the hunger pangs and I licked my chops in anticipation of a hearty breakfast in the making.

In addition, Mom refried beans in bacon drippings. Mmm! Coffee and refried bean and bacon tacos. There was no other more perfect combination of breakfast ingredients, these two were in their own food group. A mouthwatering breakfast for me! A flashing neon sign reading "La Casa de los Tacos" and "tacos to go!" should have hung outside our door. She made enough tacos for breakfast and lunch because we wouldn't be back until dark. Extra potatoes and eggs were boiled the night before and packed in dishtowels. The day's tacos she piled up high were carefully packed in miniature print-cotton cloth sacks that once held flour.

The wonderful aromas filled my nostrils as I walked out the door into the pitch dark morning-to-be. The thought of possibly eating a hot breakfast any given morning lessened the reality of the ritual of rising to face another long and arduous day. A sit down breakfast would have to wait till the weekend, today, breakfast would be served al fresco, in the field.

We moved from one field to another, but the scenery did not change – the ditches all looked the same. The sights above the ground disappeared as I stared at the mud walls –and the mud walls stared right back at me – every day. When I tried to peek over the edges of the canals, it was similar to peering through a submarine's periscope. My doe eyes scanned down the long beet rows looking for signs of life.

Rows of beets.

The foreman collected us before dawn. Because he was the one who brought us and several families in his truck to Colorado it was his responsibility to take us all to our designated fields every day. The distance between us and the other family was a couple of miles, still in the vicinity in Ovid. Because of his responsibility he got up much earlier than we did. He traveled from his place with his family, then collected the next family, then come for us. His collection time was so early that we always were ready by 4-4:30 at the latest. His truck was full of very sleepy strangers. I slept fully clothed. I'd be thrown onto the back of the truck and off to the field we'd all go in pitch darkness. We'd then wait in the shadows of the night, until the first streak of light appeared at sunrise.

I slept on the dirt covered up entirely in blankets to keep warm, until the first glistening rays began to peak. I opened my eyes to see the rays of light ever so softly coming across the horizon, defining the landscape of the fields. It was a glorious view of Earth coming to life. With just enough daylight, they'd take to the rows, I stayed in the ditch watching the sunrise.

As dusk set over the hills, everyone was dead tired, drained. When it was time to head home, I'd be the first one hoisted onto the truck. I slumped over the piled blankets, closing my eyes part of the way. As beautiful as the early morning's rays were, the sunset signaled rest to the homebound souls of the fields. In spite of the day's sunburn, heat exhaustion, and heartache, I was thankful I was going home, too, even if it was just to a house. When we saw the shadow of the house, I knew sanctuary was just minutes away.

My daily routine did not change - I slept in pants and layered flannel shirts ready for the next morning. As soon as I awoke, no time was spared, and when dropped off, I stayed by the edge of the field or in the canal, curled up in a cocoon of blankets until mid-morning when the temperature began to warm up. April and May mornings were still cold. During the day, I kept a sheet or a blanket over my head to shield myself from the sun. Eventually, Dad lent me an old sombrero. It spun around my head, but it did its job! It protected my head from sunburn. The hat's colorful crown helped anyone in the field spot me lounging in the ditch, and bobbing my head. It became my ritual of "bob and go seek." If they couldn't see me from the farthest end of the field, what difference did it make anyhow?

Sitting at the edge of the field was my amphitheater, and I held a front row seat to watch the sun peak out from the other side of the Earth, radiantly rendering a new revelation every morning. At times, clouds shrouded the golden rays, but then gave way to a background canvas of the iridescent hues of the heavens. Some morning dew patches hovered over the field, the beet leaves sparkled much the same as sequins as the sun's rays glistened through the mist. Wow! What gorgeous views, clearly seen through my tearing eyes. Magnificent and radiant are still the visions in my mind, while in the distance, two-legged beings cast shadows onto the sugar beet rows.

Three Blind Mice, Maybe Four

One day, Dad pitched a dirty ragged tarp over the ditch and set wooden stakes on each side to tie it. I could have sworn the tarp was the same one on the truck that transported us here.

A five year old could survive all day under a makeshift tent, it created a haven for a campout. It became my home for the entire day. As long as there wasn't any water flowing through the ditch, I lived under that tarp

My "daycare center" for 12-14 hours daily; a ditch with my field mice.

every day from the dreadful pre-dawn hours to dusk, until we left the field. Under it, I'd eat, play, and cry myself to sleep. If we were blessed, the field would be near a creek with magnificent shady trees, or right next to a farmer's house with mammoth

cottonwood trees centuries old. I still revere these towering giants, which provided shelter.

The tent covered me, creating a peaceful sanctuary from a blazing sun. It was the only reliable source

The faithful cottonwood trees.

for shade. Nevertheless, anytime, anywhere, along any ditch, there was always a sliver of an "island" to hold onto in my total isolation.

Occasionally, a storm breeze cooled me off after a summer's rainstorm or from a fleeting light shower, while shading under my perfect getaway "island," the ditch.

A rendering of a typical day for me in the field; left alone with the field mice as company.

My constant company was nature and the tiny field mice burrowed along the sides of the ditches. The crumbling of dried mud chunks gave away their hideouts. I grabbed them by their tails and tried pulling them out of their nesting holes, but they eluded me. To lure them out, I dropped bits of tortillas along the crumbled mud bank areas where I had spotted them digging. One sniff of food and they'd all come to the party! I gave them names like Papo, Lala, and Lulu. I remember calling out to them by these names to come out and play with me. "Ven a jugar conmigo" ("Come play with me"). I was not alone, anymore.

Since I had no toys to play with, Dad came up with an ingenious idea. He customized a hoe to fit me. With it, I helped them space beet plants, within my short distance of the rows, next to my ditch. He meticulously sanded the handle so I wouldn't splinter my hands. It was just a matter of time he began grooming his youngest "hand." Soon, I'd be initiated into his labor force full-time. I was a way to gain more ground, to clear more rows. I was needed for that reason. So, at the age of five I became a part of the working team.

As difficult as this kind of work seems for a five year old, I did not know any better. However, nothing prepared me for the daily terror of abandonment. Nothing prepared me for the suffering, the neglect or the solitude of twelve to fourteen hour days of isolation and loneliness. Moreover, the realization of those significant moments crushed the child's spirit, down to her soul. Each day I became more resigned to the inevitable, the crying gradually subsided, and I gave in to their ways. This is the way it will be. "I'm on my own to fend for myself," I thought, but the trauma became embedded.

Occasionally, a jet flew over leaving a white trail across the sky and I imagined it's me soaring to a comforting haven. Each day brought a new adventure. I found bird nests with baby chicks among the endless sugar beet rows. I didn't touch the nest for fear that the mama bird will abandon the babies leaving them to die. She could have abandoned them, as I had been. Frightened bunnies, rabbits, and squirrels scampered ahead of me as I ran through the nearby alfalfa fields. I found tons of arrowheads while walking the rows and in surrounding areas.

The sights and sounds of nature reassured and entertained me. Around me was the deep blue skies, an occasional swift shower to cool, to the sounds of birds, the earth itself, furry animals, and even the spirits of Native Americans whose arrowheads I unearth. Everything around me flourished, for it is the ideal milieu for consolation. God's creations merit reverence. Life at its purest.

A Daily Bath

By the time we got home, bathed, and ate dinner, it's time for bed, with little time left to prepare for the following day. Because Mom and my half-sister worked the fields, they weren't home to do all the pre-cooking to have supper ready when everyone got home. As soon as they arrived, they washed-up, and began cutting chicken and potatoes for the next evening's meal while cooking our nightly dinner. Stacks and stacks of tortillas were cooked fast and furious for the next day's tacos.

Since we had no water heaters, we heated up buckets of water on the stove and hauled them into the "bathing" room to bathe in galvanized washtubs. Our water well was a ways down from the house, so to get water one cranked the well handle up and down until the ice cold water flowed from underground rivers. I always needed a bath because I was a mess at the end of the day. I did whatever I wanted to while out in the fields. I was a kid, in trouble, playing in the mud. Mud was easily accessible. When water from underground rivers flowed through the ditch, an adjoining ditch was blocked off with a floodgate, and the excess water seeped into the dry canal- hello, mud heaven! While lounging under my tarp, I'd make mud castles, mud pies, mud tortillas. At times I went wild, smothering myself in the cold, mushy mud and laying out in the sun to "bake" myself--great facials before I knew about facials! My half-sister washed my hair with Prell Shampoo to get the chunks of dried mud baked into my scalp out as the scent of Palmolive soap and Prell Shampoo lingered in the room, even with holes in the wall. It was a daily chore, but oh, what a luxury.

Luckily, we stocked up on the giant green bottles of Prell shampoo and loads of Palmolive bar soap. The boys washed up and maybe washed their hair for dinner, but I don't recall if they fully bathed each night. There wasn't time. I think they bathed on Friday nights or Saturday mornings. Eventually, I learned to bathe myself. I just needed help bringing in the buckets of hot water.

On most evenings Dad and the boys sat outside soaking their tired feet, practically falling asleep with their feet still in the tubs. They regained their strength for another day. In spite of the day's laboring aches and pains, we looked forward to the evenings. Staying up slightly longer was forgiven. Since we had no electronic entertainment, not even a Philco radio, we passed our time by playing cards or listening to stories told by the boys and Dad. I mostly listen. I had no stories to tell.

Long days, too many days sunken in muddy ditches, looking up from the ditch is all I had. Stargazing became my favorite nighttime escape when the star-studded night sky lit up with a gazillion stars, as if buckets and buckets of glitter were cast into the heavens. Salvation drew closer from above. I imagined waiting for a magical flying carpet to offer me reprieve.

Suddenly, firecrackers showered the night sky with streaks of light, but the streaks were shooting stars. The meteors glowed as they burned up in a blaze of light when plunged into the Earth's atmosphere. I tried to make a wish for every one I saw. Darn, there wasn't enough time to get through one wish, let alone come up with other ones, but I made it a promising one, if that's all I got.

All of a sudden, we saw a star racing across the heavens, while others stood still. I thought it would burst into a glow similar to the others, but not this one. It was high tailing it. Later, I found out it was a satellite, a tiny spaceship, which traveled around the

Earth. Go figure. It stirred up conversations and interest as to who might be in it, if anyone. I was fortunate to see it on other stargazing nights.

Years later, I learned these tiny "ships" were called probing satellites. Perhaps as many as two circled the Earth in a race for domination by two super, worldly powers: the United States and Russia.

However, nothing as majestic rivaled the bright silver full moon. It stole the show, as its magnificent light diminished all other stars.

Sometimes the moonlight illuminated the fields, until the first streak of sunrays peered from the opposite horizon. It's by invitation only, selected souls viewed this wonder – I was one of them.

Who Wipes?

No porta potties were provided in the fields.   One either held it in or took a "dump" in one's shorts and dropped it inconspicuously somewhere out in the field. "Shake a leg, something's bound to drop." It was easier for guys to take a leak than for a woman to squat out in an open field – a woman's only choice was to go into a deep enough ditch so as to not to "moon" anyone looking in our direction.

Four years later, when we bought a vehicle ('56 aqua green Ford truck) the guys opened a door opposite the field and peed behind it. For us gals, even if we squatted behind the door, our ass appeared under the truck from far away. One could easily guess who it was by the size of the white doughy object reflected from under the truck.

Dad never complained about the lack of bathroom facilities. He figured that is just the way things are when you are a migrant laboring in unchartered territories. Maybe he feared being run off if he rocked the boat. As demoralizing as it sounds, that was our circumstances.

By 1961, we purchased a 1956 aqua green Ford pickup. I recall an incident in which I really had to go! We worked the field next to the farmer's two-story house. Bushes and trees lined the entrance of the property. Not knowing who would be home or worse yet, looking out a window from the second floor, I couldn't chance "going" in the bushes. Quick - Think! I brought a brown paper bag I found in the truck, and climbed onto the back of the pickup, and pulled down the dangling piece of tarp. I proceeded to take care of my "needs." When I finished, I climbed down with the brown bag in my hand. I managed to crawl under the pickup. When I reached the center, I started to dig with my bare hands. The ground was so compact, I decided to pull out my hoe to get through. While doing this, I scraped my knuckles and hands, because of the cramp work space between the ground and the metal thingamajig- the differential. Nevertheless, I did it! The hole was deep enough to bury the bag. I covered it best as I could and told no one. From then on, "going" was a piece of cake. I packed brown paper bags and "tush" paper. I could have coined the phrase "going green" back in the early 60s. Biodegradable!

Adventures such as these were all too common. We were the pioneering migrants whose survival depended on hurdling the insurmountable hardships we encountered. We always grasped the experience's lesson. We felt like foreigners going into those fields, yet we were right at home. Just as our Spanish ancestors did when they explored and claimed these lands more than two centuries earlier, we walked these lands, too, following their footsteps.

My Dream is Revealed-
Northward Bound, Our Adventures Begin

In the 50s, "contratistas," foremen on behalf of sugar beet farmers in Colorado, recruited Mexican-American families in the Rio Grande Valley to work the sugar beet fields. By Mexican-American, I refer to families with ancestors from Mexico who held U.S. residency and citizenship.

Migrating was already in my parents' blood when this happened. As they had already lived as nomads across South Texas. Before my birth, they lived in four different places in the Rio Grande Valley.

Is it any wonder, then, that they jumped at the chance to fulfill their dream by migrating north to find the "gold" when they were recruited in 1958? The number of persons in each household was important for the task. The more members in a family, the more the family earned, but it also meant greater profit for the foreman.

The planting of the beet crop began in early spring if the weather cooperated. This meant the farm workers were needed there by April.

Our family was recruited in April 1958. At the time, we had just moved to Edinburg. (Is this about the fifth move?) My parents, the remaining four half-brothers, my half- sister, and I began the trip, in the foreman's one-ton, green, 1950 Chevy truck. Black smoke spewed from the truck's exhaust tail pipes when it stopped just feet from the house's front entrance. The sputtering of the engine went on for another five minutes, then croaked. A great indication we're not traveling first class--rather trash class.

The dilapidated truck, held together with tape and glue, had seen better days. Moreover, dents the size of a melon were visible all around it. I tried to count them but ran out of numbers to count all the dents. The dangling pieces of bumper were tied to the frame of the truck with what appeared mangled baling wiring. Its door mirrors stuck out-way out-in spite of having just enough mirror pieces glued for the driver to view rear traffic.

Over the years, we nicknamed it "Tío Chon's," the "Bondo" truck: a remnant of a one-ton truck, smoke spewing, mosquito- killing machine on four to six slick tires, depending on the destination, that transported us "from point A to point B." No frills.

Bondo's descendant, a newer model of the truck that transported us to the fields.

I was lifted into the back under pitched tarps while several other run-down trucks waited, already loaded with other families. When we were ready, all the trucks formed a caravan of pioneer migrants heading north.

We packed only the necessities-clothing, some cooking utensils, pots, and pans-that fit in burlap sacks and cardboard boxes. We joined other families in the same truck. I remember every minute of this two-day traveling nightmare complete with rattling pots and pans, sleeping on the truck and stopping for pee breaks when the driver stopped to gas up the truck. We packed plenty of assorted tacos - beans and eggs, potato and eggs and

as my vulgar brothers joked, "papas a huevo" (forced to eat potatoes) to eat on the road. They would have to last us for at least
two days of travel time.

I can still hear the truck's engine-a deafening, ear-killing roar.
I felt the reverberation of the thundering, sputtering engine, as it
pounded my head into the size of a huge watermelon. Its engine
exhaust choked the life out of us, gasoline fumes and soot from
the double mufflers seeped through the cracked floor planks. I
could see the pavement underneath us through the warped planks.
The constant flapping of the tarps barely protected us from the
wind and sun, after a while they were shredded to pieces by the
wind. Sunburned, wind burned, windblown, and practically deaf,
we trucked on, northward.

We arrived in Ovid, Colorado in the early hours to near freezing temperatures. What a hell of a contrast to the warm, muggy
days we left behind a couple of days ago in Edinburg, Texas! To
stay warm I snuggled between my parents. In spite of all the covers on me, they still gave up their blankets to cover me. The other
families in the truck shivered while we waited for dawn and the
first glimpse of a warming sun.

Local farmers gathered at the meeting place for a chance to
claim a family. We parked off a dirt road near an open field along
with the rest of the caravan that stretched as far as I could see
if I stood on a bucket to look in all direction. Peeking through
the cracks of the warped sides of the truck, I caught a glimpse
of a miniature house made of aluminum, complete with a door. I
thought it was an outhouse, but when we were given a chance to
go pee, we found out it was an irrigation pump house.

We waited for quite some time before we were disbursed as
contracts or agreements - whatever they were- met the terms sat-

isfactory to both the farmers and "contratistas." All the while, we were still on the damn truck. At the end of the day, a Japanese farmer by the name of Tom Kobayashi, claimed us. The others were assigned to neighboring farms that needed harvest hands. Mr. Kobayashi had several hundred acres of sugar beets planted, or so I heard in conversations amongst Dad and the boys. Anyway, he wasn't the only one with that many acres. Several farmers had as much or more.

That evening, we were taken to a white wooden frame house near a hill on the outskirts of Ovid. Dad quickly fired up the dusty wood burning stove with firewood. The embers glowed brightly releasing much needed heat, as we gathered around the stove to share the warmth. The burning wood emitted a cracking sound that comforted me in this new environment far from anything familiar.

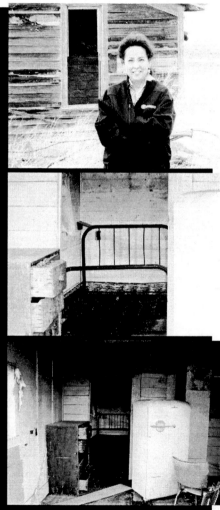

There was no indoor bathroom. The attached storage room was a "bathing" room with a dirt floor, and the outhouse was a distance from the house.

Now, back home In Edinburg, we had an outhouse, but at least it wasn't f*** cold there. I was in dire need "to go" since we had been kept aboard the damn truck

First house I ever called "home"; the Kobayashi white house still stands. – Fifty years later I visited it in 2013.

all day long until we got to Mr. Kobayashi's place. Talk about a "backed-up plumbing issue!" I managed to get to the outhouse by feeling my way with the help from a light streaming from one of the house windows. I squatted over a wooden plank, with a carved out hole while the blustering frigid winds blew up my wazoo! I kept the door open to let some light in while I completed my task, but the damn gusty winds slammed it shut. A sudden shot of terror sent my nerves into disarray. I couldn't see shit! Not being able to see, I had to assume my aim was right on target. I felt around to estimate my proximity to the "drop zone." My legs shook as I tried to keep squatting. The outhouse swayed as the wind gusts slammed the walls. Any second, I felt I would topple, shit house and all! Then, I heard some whistling sounds coming through the cracked wooden boards, I yelled out, "Alguien me está viendo!" ("Someone's looking at me!") There wasn't anyone outside the outhouse. The noise was just the blustery outbursts of very strong winds messing with me. Needless to say, I had to change my clothing from the waist down. I missed.

That night, we slept on old cots with worn out mattresses. I don't think we had bed sheets. The boys slept on rusted bunk beds in one room, while Mom, Dad, my half-sister, and I slept in the adjoining room.

The next morning, we began to settle in our new place. I think Dad was taken into town to bring whatever food supplies we needed. The home furnishings included a cast iron stove, a square wooden table and chairs, and an old icebox. It wasn't much, but at least, we had electricity.

Early In the morning, Mom reheated left over tacos on the iron griddle over the stove. Three-day old flour tortillas were a bit stiff, but I swear, her tacos had never tasted that delicious. By

then, I couldn't iden-
tify their fillings, but
we weren't about to
get choosy over left-
overs!

I explored our sur-
roundings, like any
curious five year old.
The house stood all
alone near the road,
the property had no
trees. Slightly North

David Brandt, our neighbor across the Nebraska
state line; we met for the first time in 2013.

East, just across the road from us, stood another farmhouse and
barn. I later learned who this family was, the Brandts, with the
"towering twins" of David and Dennis Brandt.

The smoke stack from our house spewed puffs of grey-black
soot. I figured Mom was just getting the "hang" of the wood
burning stove, or began sending out smoke signals for rescue or
something.

Early morning was sunny, but bitterly cold. I saw my breath,
and my nostrils twinged with the brisk thin air, both of these
things added to the excitement of a newfound land. I found it
hard to control myself. Just west of our house, were rolling hills
that looked like roller coaster mounds made of earth. From my
perspective, they appeared mountainous and grand with a white
house atop of the hills.

Gently sloping hills descended to a ribbon, lush, green, wind-
ing as far as I could see. It was the South Platte River, bordering
the rural town of Ovid, home to the Great Western Sugar Mill.

Country barns overshadowed the farmhouses. In the green-checkered squares between the farms grew alfalfa, corn, and the infamous sugar beet plants. The sugar beets overwhelming pretty much everything else.

Mr. Kobayashi's farmhouse was just a hop, skip, and a jump from ours, I was told. I soon met his family. Joyce, one of the youngest Kobayashi girls befriended me. Joyce's siblings included the eldest Kobayashi daughter JoAnne, followed by Donna and finally Carol the youngest of the girls.

I walked to their place, which was about a block directly south of their white house where we were stayed. Joyce hid behind her eyeglasses, but once we got to know each other, I learned she was witty, giggly, with a shrieking, high pitch voice. I had fun hanging around her when I had the chance.

In the stillness of that crisp cold morning, as I stood atop that hill, I spotted a flock of birds fly over me. Their chirping carried on their songs of the day. Especially moving was the sound of the Warbler, whose unique unceasing buoyant melodious sound warmed that chilly morning. Their melodies eased my fears of the unknown in this part of the new world. I felt them welcome me to Colorado.

Shitty, Shitty, Bang-Bang, Banged Up Trucks

Throughout Ovid's country/farm roads, trucks' exhaust engines disrupted the calm with sputtering, spitting oil, misfiring, and the occasional backfiring pop. This scene was common in the early morning hours, between four and five o'clock, as foremen delivered hands to the fields.

The trucks were the epitome of "shitty-shitty bang-bang, banged up" trucks that abused the farm roads daily. I laugh about it now, but back then, I cursed at them, and I'll tell you why. As the foreman's truck sputtered up to the front of the house to get us, the smoke and soot fumes killed the early morning's fresh air, not to mention our lungs. It wasn't as obvious in the morning as in the afternoon, but we could spot anyone of these trucks smoking up the roads and creating dust, traveling ten-twenty miles per hour, they couldn't go too fast on a dirt road, not that they could go faster. We'd spot "dent city" approaching, the dilapidated one with dents and dangling wired up bumpers. Yep, that's "Bondo," our ticket! It spewed black smoke about half-a-mile away clouding my beautiful sunsets.

I cursed at that truck many a times, particularly in the afternoons. We were dead tired, drained, exhausted. I didn't care if Dad heard me, because I learned the cuss words from him. I was just a child absorbing everything I heard and saw. I think he enjoyed it. I think it made him feel he had company describing the feelings of a day of hard labor, sweat, tears, aches and heartaches all mashed together and whatever else came our way.

The early round ups and late drop offs took their toll and flustered the family, especially me. Dad knew this. And, he was the first to verbalize his frustrations. Dad cussed a lot - big time.

He had a wonderful collection of descriptive cuss words, nouns, adjectives and verbs to "describe" his sentiments, such as "hay viene el hijo de la ch***!" ("Here comes this m*****f*****r!") "Hay viene el troque ch***!" ("Here comes the f****truck!") Those are just a few of his preferred, if not daily, expletives. Under our circumstances, there were very few truly happy moments. We just couldn't see anything positive at the end of the day, except letting the driver know how we felt about it. And, it wasn't this guy's fault! He just took us to and from the fields. That was the job he was paid to do. It was our choice to get on the damn truck. I know Dad realized it, too. He had no choice than get on the truck and go work, and take his family to the fields.

The picture of that truck coming down the road is still so vivid in my mind, as are the cuss words that I used to lash out, because I heard them from Dad. He was the master of cuss words, but the boys could not cuss, because they thought it would be disrespectful.

I laugh about it now, but looking back how I learned some of the best Spanish cuss words from him at a very young age. I wasn't taught how to cuss in school, that was all home-schooling: call it Pre-K Cuss 101! I wasn't slapped nor punished for cussing. It was common. If Dad blurted them, I repeated them. I just lived by example, and that was his example.

"Camp Caca" The Texas Pan Handle

1958.

Right after the beet harvest in October that same foreman lit firecrackers just short of shooting scud missiles up my family's butt, to convince them to work the cotton gins in Midway, Texas. Midway is a farming community located in the Texas Panhandle just about twenty miles from Lubbock. For this job, only the men folk were allowed work.

From Ovid, we headed south with our belongings, and gifts from the kindly Mr. Kobayashi: a burlap sack of redskin potatoes, one filled with pinto beans, and another with onions. Every year we worked for him, he always shared his crops with us. These extra food supplies would help to feed us through the harsh winter months ahead.

"Bondo" and the misfit of a driver provided our traveling accommodations in the back of the open truck. (We couldn't seem to shake this guy.)

We were taken to a camp of barracks about twenty miles from any civilization. It was a city created of elongated, narrow gray metal buildings built from corrugated tin sheets, rising from the flat, barren, and desolate countryside. From a distance it resembled a gigantic silver space ship looming over barren land, but as we approached the compound, it transformed into an unsightly, slummy monstrous fortress, embedded into the surrounding parched land, as far as the eye could see. Thinking back, this camp could have been a military complex housing soldiers eons ago. Needless to say, it was a frightening sight for this kid.

On our tail were dark, ominous clouds closing in on us, a squall of dust ahead of the wintery storm. Frigid, gusting winds swirled the rust-colored dust in our direction from neighboring fields to the north as we approached the entrance. We arrived in one of those clouds of dust. The dust triggered a coughing, choking frenzy in us that we placed bandanas over our mouths and noses to filter out as much as possible. As a result, I experienced my first micro "dust" abrasion as the fine dust sanded off my already wind burned face.

This place was arid and lifeless. With the exception of dried up twisted cotton stalks still rooted, no other vegetation thrived. The barracks, row after row, after row butted right up to the edge of the endless acres of pitifully plucked cotton stalks.

Gray, dirty cotton shreds resembled straggly human hair clinging to the dried bulbs that reminded me of shrunken heads on spears. Blustering winds proved too powerful, dislodging the dingy, white, feathery plumes floating aimlessly in sight.

We were told to select between two empty barracks to live. When we peeked in the door of the first barrack, it was unbelievable! The place was trashed. It was coated with fecal matter and had a horrendous stench of urine.

It was a nightmare of unprecedented grossness. Dad slammed the door and raised hell about the filthy conditions. His cussing could burn through ice, if there had been chunks of falling ice. We tried another barrack, several doors down which was just as bad as the first but not as smelly.

Mom poured bleach and disinfectants on the floor after sweeping out the mounds of trash. It seemed that other workers picked the cotton and lived in the barracks in the summer and often stayed through the fall. And, strangely enough, instead of using outhouses, they'd urinate and poop in the corners of non-occupied barracks.

In the barracks, there was no furniture of any kind. It did however have a grimy two-burner propane stove on a built-in wooden table nailed to the bare two by four wall stud. It also lacked running water and a shower stall. Only a frayed dangling extension cord for a single light bulb hung from the ten-plus foot ceiling.

A single water faucet found at the end of the line of barracks served the row of eight barracks. We hauled it in buckets to wash the floors. We scrubbed the floors as best we could, still we wouldn't take in our personal items until the strong odors of bleach dissipated. We left the door and the screenless wooden window open for ventilation, while the freezing winds whipped into our barrack. Unlike our personal items, and because we had nowhere to stay, we waited inside the barrack while the chemicals aired out. Tearfully, I remember this day, the stench of powerful cleansers and other noxious odors emanate a moment frozen in time.

While we waited, I got the urge to use the bathroom. I had seen the condition of these barracks up close, now it was time to go to the outhouse barracks down the row. The camp had only two outhouses, one for women, and the other for men. To me they resembled garages with a side door leading into them. Their walls were high up almost to the roof and had jagged edged windows cut out of the tin walls, for ventilation.

I grabbed a flashlight. I remember shining the light in front of me to help me make my way. As I approached the entrance of the outhouse, an unbearable, unimaginable stench overwhelmed me. Uncontrollably, I vomited and urinated over myself. Soiled in my urine, I ran back to the barrack in hysterics. No one had to ask me what happened, but I blurted out my horrifying experience. Nighttime fell by the time we moved in with our personal belongings. It was then I finally changed my clothes.

That night we slept on the cold cement floor sprawled out on blankets. Pieces of cardboards served as mattresses. We left the stove on for heat, but as the temperatures steadily dropped, water beaded from the condensation on the ceiling and began to drop on us. I remember Dad stuffing the rotted gap underneath the door that allowed the Arctic air to make its way in to us.

None of us slept because of ice-cold water drops splattering our faces, and the frigid conditions. These barracks had no insulation, they were simply made of sheet metal from top of the roof to the exterior walls.

The next morning, Dad and the boys gathered some plywood sheets and nailed them to four short stakes to build wooden beds the size of a twin bed. The beds were built low to the floor, that way if one cracked, we wouldn't have too far to fall but were at least above the lingering bleach-urine fumes. To this we piled on the blankets and quilts to finish our nice plain bed.

That one barrack didn't fit in all the beds, so the boys cut through the adjacent barrack's tin wall. Then, we carefully lifted the tin sheet just enough to crawl through it. We took care not to get cut by the jagged edges, even though it had its own front door, but it remained locked from the inside. We used that room for privacy when we changed clothes, or when it came time to sponge bathe. Nightly, two or three of the boys slept on that floor.

BE AWARE:: this "bathroom" material may not be appropriate for many to read especially those with weak stomachs.

Early the next morning, I had to use the outhouse, yet again. This time, however, Mom joined me. With daylight, everything was clearer.

A massive stench met us in the entrance. In the outhouse, there were two rows of back-to-back planks, with about twenty cut out holes to either sit on or squat. No dividers, no cover were present for privacy on any side. Mom and I watched in horror as women or kids walked in, and did their business right on the floor of the outhouse just past the entrance. Their mess left no clear walking space. To walk around, I tiptoed my way around the piles of shit. We were shocked that they preferred to poop on the ground than get on top of the planks to dump. The horrible sights and stench turned my insides out.

I also remember seeing some people carrying out potty pans, shit pans in the mornings from their barrack to the outhouse. Mom told me some preferred to go in the privacy of their barrack and dump it out the next morning. I think they felt that the planks were rotted and unsafe for anyone to squat over them, and privacy mattered, as well. Anyone who squatted over the planks to take a dump was at the mercy of everyone's entertainment. I feared walking in on anyone in the outhouse. I was embarrassed to see them even though I was a kid, I had scruples. Because of the need

At "Camp Caca:" the barracks, clothes lines swaying with the plains' wind.

for privacy, women tried to hide as they did their business in the corners.

It was insufferable to feel the humiliation of not having the privacy in those facilities. Shortly after that morning, I was given my own shit pan, and every morning I'd take it to the outhouse and, while holding my breath, dumped it into the nearest hole.

For the years we lived there, the only other standing building near us was an old rickety, grungy white, wooden church just down a ways from the road from the barracks. Thinking back, it resembled more of a chapel, a place for worship, possibly for the soldiers who may have been stationed at that camp. The church once boasted a white steeple that had rotted into a rusty, orange beacon yet, it still stood as a symbol of faith and hope for the many afflicted souls living in the foulness of that squalor of a camp.

Anglo women came by the camp. They were members of that church and brought gifts, such as clothing, some blankets, and food items. They didn't bring much to satisfy the many families in the barracks, but every bit helped. They gave me some corduroy pants and a couple of sweaters. They also befriended some of the kids and took us to that church for services during the day and treated us with Kool Aid and cookies afterwards. I went just to check out the situation, and for the Kool Aid and cookies. I'm sure the other kids went for the sweet treats, too.

A corner of the church was covered in mounds of musty-smelling, used clothes, and all sorts of used kids' toys. We were forced to color for hours until we had crayons sticking out of our ears, bored out of our gourd! As for the girls, they made us play with dolls found in the pile of broken toys. We'd take a short break, then, they read us passages of scripture from the Bible, followed by songs played on the piano, a sing along. One of the songs I learned, and still remember was "Jesus loves me, yes I know, 'cause the Bible tells me so." I loved it, even if I only learned that one line to sing, I figured God heard me. We kids didn't care about the songs, we just rambled on like a bunch of idiots pretending we knew all the words, but the ladies applauded us as we sang our hearts out. Kool Aid and cookies were the payoff. Afterwards, they walked us across the road to the barracks, and we scurried into our respective rat holes.

I didn't want to make friends with any of the kids living there, in my eyes, I was a loner, and preferred it that way.

By the calendar, we spent many Thanksgivings and Christmases in the barracks for several years. I use those terms now, but didn't know the holidays existed until years later because my family didn't celebrate either day.

Thanksgiving came and went without us knowing about turkey, and giblet gravy or pumpkin pie. We had a pot of beans, and hot tortillas. My parents did not put up a Christmas tree, nor decorate the front door with lights. Nothing. The gifts I received, if any, came from donations from that church's congregation which brought gifts for the kids. But, if I wanted to get something, I'd better be in front of the line when the ladies came bearing gifts. Most of the time, I didn't show up for the donations.

While Dad and the boys worked the cotton gins those three months, I felt like a prisoner in the barracks. I was forced to stay inside because of blizzards common during that time. Because of the lack of insolation and the wintry air coming in from the wooden door cracks in the barrack I'd stay wrapped in blankets day and nights.

We nailed cardboard around the edges of the window to try to keep the cold out. Old blankets remained nailed to the inside of the decayed wooden door to cover the cracks. On these subzero nights, no one really had a restful sleep because of the freezing cold droplets of water constantly pelting our faces. I tried to keep warm curled up under a pile of blankets, but my body stiffened and ached from the extreme cold. I am sure the rest of the family members endured the agony of those frigid, sleepless nights, too.

We kept the burner on twenty-four hours a day, so the condensation was as constant as the aroma of pinto beans cooking. On occasion, we had a sunny day, but still maintained frigid temperatures.

These had been the most deplorable living conditions in which I ever lived. We returned to the camp three more winter seasons. I look back at my time spent in these barracks and imagine myself as a prisoner of war living in concentration camps which were truly unfit for human beings. How could so many displaced families live in such inhumane and hellish conditions? More importantly why, why would Dad subject us to three months living in torturous, frozen dungeons and come back again for three more years?

.... Give Us This Day Our Daily Tortilla and Beans

We lived about twenty miles from civilization. The foreman took us into the nearest town to buy groceries. We didn't have the privilege of charging them as we had done in Ovid, therefore our groceries shopping was minimal. Few items made it into the shopping cart, of these items most were canned goods and boxed items which included my corn flakes with the red–crested rooster painted on the front of the box. On the shopping list, flour, shortening, and coffee were a must. Food items which required refrigeration were simply not purchased since we had no refrigerator. When we purchased meat, it would be cooked and eaten the same day, with eight hungry people, not even a spoonful was spared.

I drank evaporated canned milk, "Pet" straight from the can because I had no choice. Somehow, I managed to down the corn flakes with it, in spite of its nasty taste. If any was left over, the coffee drinkers drank it, but I would have killed for some fresh "refrigerated" homogenized milk!

Food preparation happened day-to-day. With only two burners, Mom cooked a pot of beans all the time then added whatever she mustered up for the main course on the other burner. The menu included potatoes with scrambled eggs, or canned meat byproducts was sliced, fried, and stuffed into the tortillas, then rolled into tacos. A steaming bowl of soupy beans complimented the tasty fried "meat."

At any time of the day, weather permitting, we didn't mind leaving the barrack's door opened, but at dinner time the aroma of beans cooking in ours as well as in neighboring barracks was overwhelming- we coined the slogan: "Beans, it's what's for dinner!"

I came across some old photos, taken shortly after our arrival that first year. A picture speaks a thousand words, evoking so many memories in detail - - the clothes lines in the background, swaying with the plains' winds, and the barracks up against the fields- the details rushing back.

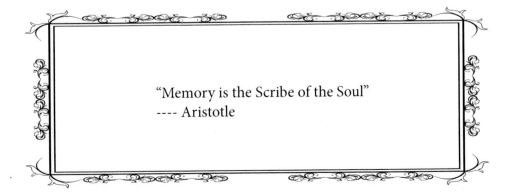

"Memory is the Scribe of the Soul"
---- Aristotle

Second Verse, Almost the Same as the First

The following year I turned seven. Oh, what a year! Again, we battled the weather, the nasty barracks, and the outhouse situation. Every year we were right back to cleaning out trash, shit, and more shit! My seventh year of life was also my second year of imprisonment.

Shortly after arriving, some lice infested kids living in the next row of barracks befriended me. No sooner had I met them, then I became infected with lice. It was impossible to avoid those critters, unless one lived in total isolation. The case was so horrid, it came with constant itching and scratching. Red welts formed around my neck from my constant scratching, but I also felt them all over my body, or it just seemed that way.

Out of the three months, I remained locked up for about a month. Mom kept me in isolation. I did not get close to any family member, not that it mattered to any one of them. Playing outside, regardless the weather was forbidden. Again, we were right in the middle of winter storms that showered snow, sleet, and slush over us but, I looked forward to a sunny day, when I could at least stand by the doorway and soak up the sun's rays. I remember the sun's warmth and my forehead absorbing the energy.

Meanwhile, the ongoing scalp treatment Mom used was a stinky tincture. It burned my scalp, irritated my eyes, and its smell made me nauseous. I screamed the moment she applied the stuff with cotton balls. I whimpered for a long time afterwards, and then throw up from the lingering toxic smell.

There was no escape from that frigid, filthy, foul-smelling hell hole of a barrack!

I draped blankets around myself to keep warm and remained

isolated. While living there, I don't remember bathing once that year, but every so often Mom washed my hair, then reapplied the tincture a few days later. When my lice situation was finally over, I was still traumatized from its effects. I remained nauseous and continued vomiting. The lingering scent of that gunk left me feeling horrible from, it could have been a deadly treatment.

What a torture! I remember being just plain miserable and so desolate from this physical abuse and emotional abuse. All that started when I suffered the abandonment in the irrigation ditches in Colorado. There, at least, I had sunshine and a blue sky. I envisioned those skies and the soothing meadowlarks' melodies to get me through this ordeal.

Christmas came around, or so I think, because I heard about it in conversation. But, we had no Christmas tree, no lights, and no presents. Nada-Nada, enchilada! It just wasn't done. The constant survival mode, my family's gypsy life was only to keep moving from one work place to another. No time for any celebration, or the means to celebrate existed in their eyes. However, Dad must have felt some sympathy for me for the tortures I went through.

One morning, I woke up next to a raggedy burlap sack, tied with a piece of string and a crumpled brown paper bag. I sat up quickly opening both. The burlap bag contained whole pecans, and the brown bag had mini peppermint candy canes. This was my Christmas gift! I grabbed the rolling pin and started smashing the nuts. It was the first time I'd ever eaten pecans or peppermint candies. Instinctively, I chunked the two together and felt my nostrils twinge with the peppermint spice. The sweetness of the mint and mixed pecans was ideal, the crunch was the best!

This became a family tradition. Dad bought peppermint candy

canes and pecans every Christmas after that. For me, it was better than receiving nothing at all. I have memories of him shelling the nuts and handing me the halves. I'd pop them in my mouth along with a chunk of candy. Total bliss found in my prison. I feel the tears well up in my eyes now. All I needed was a simple treat to get me though those harsh times. This one kind gesture eased my sufferings, at least for a moment.

Every Christmas, I celebrate that special memory of him by shelling pecans and eating them with peppermint candy canes. When I do this, all these memories flood my thoughts like they are deeply etched in my heart as well.

Aside from these grim-telling ventures, life went on for the miserable. Mom washed our clothes in tubs of freezing water. To dry them, she hung clothes on make-shift rope clothes lines we placed from corner to corner in the adjacent barrack where the boys slept. The clotheslines provided by the camp were far away from our section of barracks, and while she used them when the weather permitted, but she feared our clothes getting stolen. She also turned one of the beds into an ironing board to make us look presentable.

I hardly saw the boys or Dad since they worked the night shifts and often worked double shifts. The last cotton harvest took the longest to complete because some fields were so far away from the only gin still operational. For one last "sweep," distant farmers raced against time and the elements to harvest the last of the feathery plumes. I never understood clearly what Dad and boys did at work. I think they stood on top of platforms as they held and guided huge suction hoses to vacuum the cotton from trucks idling below. Drivers with their trucks loaded with cotton waited in line for their turn to pull up under these suction hoses to deliver tons of cotton still to be milled. When the last of the cotton had been harvested, the maintenance and cleaning of the machinery followed. Dad and his sons did the detailed scrubbing, lubricating, and storing of the heavy duty machinery. This gave extra work for them through mid-January.

About a mile away from the barracks, I recall seeing the gins where they worked. I especially remember how they looked at night when they were lit up as though a city of their own. The powerful night lights affixed atop the exterior of the metal buildings clearly lit the outer perimeter of the hanger-like buildings which enclosed the machinery, but once the daylight came the buildings practically disappeared from sight. They were often shrouded by dust storms or sometimes blizzards.

There was even an antiquated coffee shop just a short distance from them. I think it had been there since the beginning of time. I still remember it as if it were only yesterday. The lit up sign announcing they were "OPEN" was barely visible through the cemented grime on the window. The torn screen door hung off its hinges leading a person to its scruffy looking décor. In this café, bar stools lined the counter, as dingy ceramic coffee cups which were once white matched saucer plates piled on the tables that added to the unpleasant ambience. I paid no mind to how it looked inside; I took my chances with their food as did the workers who ate there between the extra shifts.

When I was older, and the weather permitted, I at times walked to the coffee shop just to buy a generously piled high slice of their homemade apple pie or my favorite one, coconut cream pie. I am licking my "chops" as I write.

By the time I returned to the barrack, I'd completely licked the paper plate clean, not one coconut flake was left. It took me a while to save up twenty five cents for that special treat, but then I had lots of spare time to keep working at it. I earned my treat by swiping the unclaimed pennies I found in my half-brothers' pants pockets.

One time, I found a dime along the gravely, dusty road on the outskirts of the camp on my way to the coffee shop. My find glistened with the sun, nearly blinding me. Quickly, I scooped it up. A shiny dime had dropped from heaven. I was thankful for my found treasure! Now, I needed to work harder to find the extra fifteen cents for my next getaway to "pie land." If they didn't fall from heaven, well, back to my scheme of going through the boys' pants pockets.

By now, the long hours and the hardships of the gypsy life took a toll on the whole family. This year was my half-sister's second and last visit to "Camp Caca." She met some guy there and eloped with him to escape. And the boys, they would follow soon afterwards. But, I was the only one trapped.

Tornado Alley - Colorado

Dodging golf-size hail, ice-cold rain, and wind was common. We were right in the middle of tornado season when we encountered our first adventure. Soon after the first few weeks after our arrival, a gray narrow funnel cloud began to descend close to our field. I heard the thunder over us, a loud rumbling shook the ground. I stared up at the dark clouds looming, practically on the ground. We scattered just like mice and ran for cover-jumping into the irrigation ditches. Thankfully, the scrawny-looking funnel cloud shifted away from us, but hung in mid-air. While it didn't touch the ground, the churning winds, rain and dust enveloped us. The smell of the dampness of the earth lingered.

We watched in awe as God unleashed His wrath. While it spun away immediately, we were still drenched in torrential, soaking rain. A glorious rainbow emerged from the dismal, overcast sky as if to remind us of His creations, both frightening and trusting. I believe there were countless rainbows, a blessing at the end of each storm. I must have seen a million of them in my lifetime.

"Tornado Alley" as it was later referred to by meteorologists defines the area including Colorado, Kansas, Oklahoma, and Nebraska where tornadoes and damaging storms mainstreamed in spring and summer causing major destruction in their paths.

Spontaneously, clouds formed and we knew a whopper of a storm brewed just above them. A calm, picture-perfect day was interrupted by the formation of ominous clouds appearing out of nowhere. When the clouds formed, a single thought raced through our minds – RUUUNNNN! As rain sheets descended over the field, we scattered, running for cover, but there wasn't anywhere to go.

Occasionally, storm showers popped up and we were caught in the middle of the field with no shelter. Soaked by the rains, we moved to the edge of the field to wait it out. By the time the foreman realized we were in a downpour, it would be over.

If the ground was saturated by the rains, we couldn't go back into the rows, so we waited until the foreman returned to get us. We drip-dried ourselves with the cool breeze while we waited. Other times, the cool showers cooled us off-right on time to ease the heat of the day, and we continued to work. No matter what the weather, the foreman always got us at sundown.

The most dangerous part of the storm was the lightning. Everyone buried the metal portion of their hoe into the ground for fear of attracting any lightning strikes. Hell, no, we didn't want to be fried!

When the torrential storms hit, we huddled at the edge of the field. The boys' Levi jeans and cotton long sleeve blue shirts got sopping wet and spattered with mud. Mom's and my half-sister's work hats were similar to the early women settlers' sun bonnets with the long front beaks and ties under the chin. Their hats drooped with the weight of the soaking rains. As for me, I thoroughly enjoyed the soaking rains and playing in the mud - what kid doesn't.

Meanwhile, we should have carried bars of soap on us, "we'd done had our baths" and it wasn't even Saturday.

Night storms were typically more terrifying. We'd wake up to the rumbling sounds of thunder and blustering winds and ran down to the cellar, not knowing in which direction the storms would hit. Too often, we slept in the cellar fearful of storms looming over the area.

Tea for Four – A True Fairytale

In the late 1950s and 60s when my family worked the sugar beet fields in Ovid, Colorado, Mother Nature's perils were imminent. During the spring and summer months, the unpredictable atmospheric changes were an ever present danger, as we dodged hail, ice-cold rain and blustery wind caused by thunderstorms. But, fiercely regarded were the tornados spawned spontaneously from within the storms. Their only reason for existence was to destroy anything in their path.

For our protection, we tried to shield ourselves crouched in the irrigation ditch, a place all too familiar to me. There, the rest of the family members and I hunkered down to await the outcome of the tempest.

At a very young age, I believed God unleashed his wrath in storms to remind us of His creations, both frightening and trusting. But, to comfort a terrified little girl, He painted her something truly special. Rainbows.

Rainbows appeared by the hundreds throughout all those years, usually after a spring or a summer's rain storm. I was drawn to them for their brilliant and mystical arched pathways that would magically transport me to any number of imaginary kingdoms, complete with Neapolitan-flavored ice cream-filled ditches, topped with giant, sweet strawberries. Whipped cream was optional.

Early on, I found myself sliding over one so intense in radiance, and landing on an enchanted panorama, close to the edge of the South Platte River. There, the most beautiful cotton wood trees with mystical powers created a haven for playing. The forest seemed to line the entire perimeter of a farm house. The secluded area provided a hide-away just for me!

When I was seven and the third year we migrated, we still didn't have a vehicle of our own. We were dropped off with our food and water at a farm close to the sloping banks of the river. The trees had been the tallest, with thicker trunks and the biggest, shiniest leaves ever (I suppose they benefited from the proximity of the river's moisture). I was so intrigued, just sitting under the abundance and thickness of their shade. I stayed close by shading myself, as the rest took to the fields, thinning the rows that ran north and south, slightly sloping down to the very edge of the bank.

As God is my witness, right by one of the tree's trunk I found a set of children's play dishes neatly placed over a tablecloth-a dish set for dainty girls with swirls of blue with yellow flowers depicted in the center of the plates. Matching tea cups, saucers and cream/sugar dispensers added to the colorful spread. Forks and knives were also carefully aligned to complete the setting. The whole set was identical to the grown-ups' version that I saw displayed in a fancy store's window.

Someone was about to have a tea party. "What if I am invited to attend?" I thought. I felt underdressed, but certainly I could have played the role of a pint-sized vagabond with my dirt-smudged face, knotted hair, and dusty bottom. I was excited to meet new playmates.

After I'd done my share of hoeing for the morning, I returned to sit under the trees guarding our food and water. A couple of hours passed. I stayed away from the tea setting which was about three trees away. Meanwhile, I kept my hopes up that someone would claim their "reservation" for a perfectly set tea party.

Sure enough, three little girls came from the house. They made their way down the dirt road entrance towards me, or rather to the tea setting. As they approached, I made out their ages. One looked about three, the next about five or six, and the eldest may have been about nine years old. They were dressed in their summer best: white pinafores, pink shorts, and sandals. As they approached, they stared at me, surprised that another being sat under their trees. I looked at them wondering if they're going to run me off. Where would I go? I had to stay around their place, as my family was working their field.

They came up to me and started talking. Their wavy locks of curls skimmed their clean smiling faces. They were such beautiful girls. All three talked at the same time, I tried to make out what each said. I understood some of the words. I know they asked what I was doing there. I responded "working….. my father…. Mother." I tried to speak English so they wouldn't ask me to leave. My sign language kicked in and with their gestures, I understood they were inviting me to tea. So, I followed them. They carried orange juice in a glass container and another beverage in a jar and a paper bag.

We sat across from each other on the ground, but I worried their delicate outfits would soil. They poured juice into the cups, and pulled out cookies from the paper bag. The cookies were placed onto the smaller plates. The girls displayed such prim and proper table manners: they sipped from the tiny cups, and chewed on their cookies taking tiny bites. I paid close attention to learn their "delicate," lady-like mannerisms, which were quite the opposite of mine. I was used to grabbing a flat, cold taco from the cloth bag, chunking it down, and drinking water out of a dented tin cup. Done!

We enjoyed that morning's gathering under the trees. It was

a delightful "impromptu meeting" of destiny.   I was so lucky. We feasted on orange juice and cookies and chattered on as the neighborly squirrels who lived in the enchanted cottonwood tree "forest" who understood each other's gibberish, the charismatic language of friendship spoken in a magical kingdom, somewhere near the Ovid realm. I offered my name, and to this day I remember all their names started with the letter "c."

The whole incident captivates me to this date. The idea that I came across young children who wouldn't shy away from a stranger such as me was delightful and by far the most enjoyable time I had at any place, up until then. Those were kids my age who accepted me for who I was. I learned a valuable lesson all on my own from this fortunate encounter--when friendship turns up unexpectedly, be open to receive it because magic is what you make of what's given.

The invitation, the ambiance, and the "proper setting" made it even more unforgettable. I had just starred in my first fairytale, over *one* of the rainbows.

"The Blessed Mother Teresa was Mother to the world; then, why can't she be a Saint to the world? Pray for her Canonization."
---- Emma Gonzalez

The Yellow House

Mr. Kobayashi's yellow house; missing my "red" swing!

In 1960, we still lived on Mr. Kobayashi's property. It was our third year working for him and the second house we moved to was a yellow frame house. It was just a few yards away from the white house we had occupied the year before. In front of the house were sugar beet fields, cornfields, and to the west some alfalfa fields. I remember seeing fat, furry critters--prairie dogs and the mounds of dirt they'd frantically mustered up. Any given day, several mounds popped up overnight right in front of our front door. When I stood above their burrow, I heard their squeaking underground. We threw food crumbs down and that drew them even closer to the house. They were our house pets, who greeted us when we came home. They multiplied like rabbits, so we had a whole passel of them.

The yellow frame house sat to the furthest north of the field, just a few feet from the road, facing south. An irrigation canal separated the house and the edge of the road. In actuality, the road itself was the state line between Colorado and Nebraska. A couple of mature cottonwood trees shaded the narrow backyard and a "red" wooden swing hung from one of the trees' thickest limbs - - I "lived" on that swing. This house was much roomier than the white one, but had no indoor plumbing. We still needed to use a drafty outhouse. It was here that I finally figured out why they were so drafty. The wooden planks were spaced out intentionally for airing out the building. There was no need for "Febreze" in those days.

The entire family migrated there that year. With five men, Mom, my half-sister and me in the household, there was plenty of household work to get done. We cooked, washed, and ironed. Since I was a bit older I was assigned domestic chores.

Because we had no washers, and public laundry mats were not yet available, we did our laundry by hand in galvanized bath-ing tubs. Mom poured soap in the tubs and I'd stir up the water around to make it sudsy. She heated up buckets of water to wash the white stuff and use cold water to rinse. The hardest labor other than fieldwork was doing the laundry by hand.

I helped wash the shirts because I could handle them since they weren't as bulky as the jeans. We had two washboards. Mom scrubbed the guys' jeans on one of them and I'd lend a hand on the other to wash the shirts. I'd take a sudsy shirt, slap it onto the washboard inside the tub and run it up and down over the grooves of the board then I flipped it over and repeated the same action until both sides got at least five or ten minutes of scrub-bing. Afterwards, I wrung the soap out of them, then threw them into a tub of clean water to rinse them. Dunking them in and out of the tub in ice-cold water was fun and I practically dunked my-self in it. Wringing out the excess water was not so easy. Then, I managed to hang the shirts on the clothesline to drip dry.

At the end of a wash, my knuckles were bruised and scraped. That's all I could do to help her. The time between washes was short, so, soon I was back helping her again. I noticed that Mom took the brunt of the entire load, because of this her hands and knuckles were scraped and bruised far worse than mine.

At eight years old, some of my other chores and responsibili-ties, aside from working in the fields, included cleaning, mop-ping, doing the laundry, making tortillas. I watched her cook so I learned to cook one or two main dishes that she's famous for. She cooked beans adding just the right touch of spices for the most flavorful beans in the state. She did the same thing with the tortillas, not everybody developed that extra flavor in the dough ingredients or made them come out as puffy and so soft to roll up. We couldn't eat just one.

Peace for a Beauty Queen

Our contact with the outside world, from within the long beet rows in Ovid, Colorado, was practically nil. Most migrant families, including ours had no telephone, television, newspaper, nor radio to hear any news. For that, we used old fashion, old school letter writing. From time to time, Mom received letters from estranged family members I didn't know yet and some from her neighbor friends in Edinburg.

Occasionally, she received letters from Mexico, where her relatives lived, including my Grandmother Lina, an Apache-descendant, and the only grandmother I ever knew. Mom wrote to Grandmother Lina all the time. I remember her reading all the news from Altamirano, Tamaulipas, a quaint village near the Rio Grande River, where most of the Ornelas clan lived close to her. A passel of Ornelas' sons and daughters and their families' families lived in thatched roof homes with mud walls in close proximity to each other. A letter received from the only daughter living in the U.S. stirred up quite an excitement amongst all of them. Mom's sisters would write on behalf of Grandma Lina who dictated what she wanted to tell my Mom, her only daughter living a migrant life in the U.S. Any new adventures Mom encountered along the gypsy way of living were reported back home to the whole "familia."

In 1960, when we lived in Kobayashi's yellow house, we received letters, from our Edinburg neighbors. The letters included newspaper clippings of a scandalous murder which took place in the city of McAllen, in April of that year. This happened shortly after we left for Ovid to work the beet fields. McAllen, Texas was about eight miles from Edinburg, the town we "wintered" for a spell each January after we left "Camp Caca" in the Texas Pan Handle.

In retrospect, I only listened to what Mom read in the letters and what my half-brothers tried to translate into Spanish from the English newspaper clippings that detailed the incident, as the case developed. Over a period of several months, long past the summer, we received updates on the case. It was riveting to hear bits and pieces of what Mom read from the neighbors' letters, it added to the intrigue. It seemed strange to hear of such an atrocity occurring so far away in the Rio Grande Valley. It was in sharp contrast from all the other family news on the daily lives and survival of our relatives living in Mexico. Most of the time, I listened for a second or two but if it was related to this story I ran outside so as to not listen to the gripping details which played out over and over.

As I recall, a young lady named Irene Garza had gone to confession at a Catholic church in McAllen, Texas. After she entered the church, she was never heard from until her body was discovered in a canal days later. Pieces of her clothing and personal items were found scattered on a farm road. As the story unfolded, allegedly, the main suspect was the church's priest.

I didn't know about priests or their role in the Catholic Church so when I first learned that the suspect was a priest I had no feelings about it. I first attended a Catholic church when I was ten or eleven years old. I was sent there to study in Bible class to make my first communion. It was then, when I finally met one or two of the priests at Sacred Heart Church in Edinburg, Texas. Even then, I still had no understanding of their role in the church.

However, I believed in "Dios," (God) as my mother always called to him to guide us every year we migrated to and from the work locations. I figured he was everywhere we were, because I don't recall ever entering a church just to pray. "Dios" and I became tight even after the migrating years were over. After all, I was paying some attention to our daily migrant living. If Mom was sure that this "Dios" looked out for us, well, then, why wouldn't He look after me too? The English translation I would learn in school for Dios was "God" which is the name I chose to use when I addressed him. Close to Him, I felt His presence in the fields with me, and in my simple daily thoughts. I definitely had many special requests for Him, especially to "bail" me out of the daily grind of the migrant life from the forsaken ditches to the hopelessness of no future. He nurtured the pioneering spirit of this young migrant child as she matured.

As for the murder case, I do not remember if we ever received a clipping of any arrest. We lost track of time, as we continued our gypsy life moving from one work place to another. As a result of all these moves our mail delivery was delayed and at other times was not even received.

50 years later no arrest has been made. It has, however, become the most notorious, unsolved murder case in the history of the Rio Grande Valley.

Decades later when the case was reopened for further investigation, with both new and old evidence, I worked for the District Attorney's Office of Hidalgo County as the Crime Victims' Coordinator, advocating and assisting victims of crime. Hidalgo was the county that had jurisdiction over the case. When I heard this case would be reopened, I became emotionally overwhelmed when I realized where I was the first time I heard about it. I recalled the details of the case and they instantly took me back to Ovid, Colorado where I was an eight year old migrant whose family read newspaper clippings that were mailed to us.

My life had made a complete circle. I returned to Edinburg, and in a twist of fate, was employed in a position assisting and advocating for victims of crime. Had the crime happened during my tenure as victims' advocate, I would have been the one to help her family overcome the tragedy. I felt an unfathomable sympathy for Irene's family because they were victimized for a second time as a result of the reopening of the case.

Once more, I revisited snippets of her story, and the life of Irene

Garza. She was a former beauty queen, an educator, and overall an innocent person with a strong faith in God. She is not forgotten, if we keep her in our hearts and in this vignette, she will be remembered long after the ink fades away. Her angelic name "Irene" in Greek mythology means "goddess of peace." She has earned that title too since she lives in everlasting peace and her soul radiates that perpetual peace to comfort us all.

Tortilla Heaven

Mom assigned me the "easier tasks" when I was eight years old. She lectured me in Spanish: "Te vas ha enseñar hacer tortillas." ("You're going to learn how to make tortillas.") As a result, I made tortillas every day, a huge stack.

We fed five men, who ate three to four tortillas each, at every meal. You do the math! That meant we went through lots of 25 pound sacks of flour. The flour sack was made of cotton cloth print that later became part of my wardrobe. Because it would later become a part of my wardrobe, I made sure *I* was the one to select sacks with decent prints because I knew sooner, not later, I'd be wearing it.

To make the tortillas, she mixed the ingredients, flour, shortening, baking powder, salt, and then added very warm water to mix it all up in a huge aluminum bowl. She whipped and whipped, mixed and mixed, then scraped off the edges of the bowl getting every bit of flour mixed into the big ball of dough. She patted it several times until the consistency was ready to roll out the "torts" (short for tortillas). We covered the dough with a dish towel and let it sit for a few minutes. Then, she'd start to pinch chunks of dough to make the round balls. We stacked them all around the inside of the bowl to air out, then roll them out on the cutting board. My chore for the tortilla making was to make the round balls of dough.

Since I couldn't reach the table to roll them out with the rolling pin, Dad built me a custom step-up work stool to help me get the job done. As always, he made sure we all contributed to do our share of labor, one way or another. I stood on the stool and easily reached the top of the table which was just slightly below my waist so that I could lean entirely over it and put my mighty strength and weight on the rolling pin to roll out them "torts." I hung them over on the edge of the bowl so Mom could grab them and slap them on to the griddle. She flipped the tortillas once or twice and they'd be cooked and placed on dish towels on the table to cool off.

The aroma of fresh, hot tortillas filled the house. I snuck me a tortilla with chunks of butter in it and rolled it into a burrito. The melted butter dripped all over my blouse, but oh-hh... De-li-cious! "Mexican Ambrosia!" "Eat your heart out, Zeus!" Down the hatch! By the time we were done with one of those big bowls of dough, we had cranked out 60 to 100 tortillas (minus my share!).

She had all the fillers ready to stuff the tortillas. Using three or four ingredients, she mixed potatoes/eggs, beans/eggs, bacon/eggs, potatoes/eggs/ beans, or potato/eggs/ bacon. It was a daily cornucopia of tacos. She tossed in some chopped up chili peppers, chopped tomatoes, and onions to make spicy-hot tacos for the boys.

Dinner's menu changed a bit from the daily tacos. For dinner, she cooked a "guisado," (stewed meat) or chicken in spices of garlic, cumin, ground pepper, chopped onions, chopped tomatoes, and any seasonal vegetable such as zucchini, squash, or green beans. And the aroma from cooking with all those spices and fresh, hot tortillas would have had me drooling. Mercy!

She'd get a head start by making as many tortillas as possible for a day and a half. It was a killer standing by the hot stove flipping them, a lot of work- similar to baking loaves of bread, except these were stacks and stacks of flour tortillas.

It was my designated chore, though not by choice, I want to make that perfectly clear!

Have Truck Will Travel

As I mentioned by 1961, we purchased a used 1956 aqua green Ford pickup. The boys built the sides of the bed out of wooden planks, but no roof. Weathered, tattered tarps shielded us from some of the elements, at least partially. We began our annual trips to Colorado in it, trailing the rest of the caravan of trucks full of migrant workers.

I discovered my greatest entertainment up until that time. It was KOMA-AM radio out of Oklahoma City. Every chance I had, I rode shotgun in that truck's front seat and we jammed to the early years of rock and roll music. I was hooked on rock and roll music: Chuck Berry, The Platters, Frankie Lymon, Buddy Holly, Richie Valenz, The Big Bopper, Elvis, The Everly Brothers, and on and on. The harmonizing of notes lifted me to a euphoric state of mind that put me over the moon, never wanting to return to reality.

To ride upfront with the entertainment readily available at my fingertips, I fought off everyone else slapping anyone's hand if they tried to touch the dial. My misbehavior and punishment were not taken lightly. But you see, no one messes with Rock and Roll music and gets away with it! This is the other world that sustained me. For this, I took my chances of getting my ass thrown in the back of the truck for the remainder of the trip. The adults did not realize the long stretch of miles was anything but entertaining for me. But, music numbed the "antsiness" in me, as I endured the journey.

In the evenings, we sat outside, like before, but could now listen to KOMA-AM radio until the battery died. We opened up the doors, roll down the windows, and listen to these unforgettable classics, while star gazing on the truck's hood. The songs and lyrics became my lullabies. The boys had to charge up the battery early next morning by using one of the farm trucks or tractors.

Rock and Roll music blaring from the truck's speakers was our only source of entertainment in the weeknights. That radio frequency was heard as far south as the Texas Pan Handle. It had a powerful wattage, twenty-four hours a day.

...Well, It's Saturday Night and I Just Got Paid

As an adult, I watched the movie "Hoosiers," which takes place in the 1950s. The town's scenery in the movie made me reminisce of Ovid. The historic Main Street in Ovid was the hub for all the mercantile in a two-block area. The general store, in fact the whole downtown with its gray-weathered aged buildings, were something out of an old storybook.

We shopped for our weekly groceries on Saturday. I remember entering Mr. Jonkovsky's store, as though if it were yesterday.

My eyes boggled at the sight of the tall candy-filled glass jars with treats available for the one-cent. The sign pasted on the jar screamed the bargain, ready to bamboozle anyone with a sweet tooth and for a penny you could not go wrong. Drool City! The counter receded with strategically placed jars brimming at the top with penny candy to get the easy ones on impulse surely, to get the last of your change.

The deep rectangular ice cream freezers with the glass doors that slid to the top or sideways were jam-packed with tempting ice cream delights in sundry flavors. I peered through the glass to select before opening it, all the while drooling over it, as I tried to make up my mind. If only I could get my hands on every single flavor! That was always the game plan concocting in my brain! Take all that I could!

Squeaky floors buckled under the weight of the grocery cart as one strolled up and down the aisles of goods. We found just about EVERYTHING in that store.

The building was sectioned into two areas, the main entrance was the grocery store, and the addition opened to the general mercantile side. If we were looking for dry goods, such as clothing, housewares, and farm supplies - this was the place. I recall tall, wooden tables displaying clothing, such as denim jeans and work shirts sectioned off into the different sizes. A stack of shiny galvanized buckets lit a corner of that section. All kinds of hoes were stacked against another corner.

Mom walked the aisles of canned goods and boxed items. She purchased twenty-five pound sacks of white flour bagged in printed cotton cloth sacks, later those sacks served as the fabric of some of my wardrobe. Our usual list of groceries included two of those twenty-five pound bags of flour, shortening, coffee, milk, some poultry, and scant red meat. She claimed meat was too expensive, and would not even be charged to the account because eventually we would have to pay for it.

And, who could forget the Kool Aid packages? The store owner sold ten packages for fifteen cents or less. We purchased packages of cherry, orange, lime, and grape flavors, and ten pound bags of sugar. Talk about liquid diabetes in a pitcher!

Mr. Kobayashi's generosity provided us with sacks of redskin potatoes, pinto beans, and onions he kept in underground cellars to keep from spoiling. I think he might have given us some eggs from his own chicken coups.

Mr. Jonkovsky, the storeowner, allowed us to charge our groceries with a guaranty from the foreman to pay as advancements were allotted to us. When time came to pay, we were left with less money.

Nonetheless, it didn't stop me from getting MINE! I figured I worked, too, fools! Where is my pay? I'm getting mine. Well, it came in the form of sneaking in a box of Devil's Food Cakes. These babies were packaged in green boxes, my eyes scanned the shelves like lasers zeroing in for the delectable find. The cookies had marshmallow as a shell over a chocolate cookie filling, then were drenched in creamy chocolate icing. So "devilish" tasting! If I missed out on getting a whole box of Devil's Food Cakes, then, Moon Pies filled my being. Not only were they twice the size of the cookies, they were sold individually, too. Grabbing a handful of Moon Pies added up to twice as many cookies! It was all about the economics of getting the most when they (my parents) weren't watching closely the checkout counter. And, how could I forget pigging out on ice cream popsicles? I sampled several flavors at a time. I'd place the wooden popsicle sticks on the counter to be accounted for, the stains on the sticks indicated the flavors of popsicles I had devoured in a very short period of time.

We only went into town once a week, so I made sure to make the most of it and get all that I could. It was too long of a spell from one Saturday to the next.

Then, an addiction began, when I discovered the Reese's Peanut Butter Cups. The orange squared wrappers were stacked neatly in their own box atop old wooden shelves and were welcome sights each Saturday. I had stumbled upon a food group all on its own. In my opinion, they should have been at the top of the food pyramid!

The five straight days filled by over twelve hours of slumbering in ditches, yanking mice tails, hoeing itty bitty green looking, insignificant plants took its toll on me. But every week, the Reese's Peanut Butter Cups in those orange and brown wrappers were a sight for my sore eyes, Halleluiah! Salvation and redemption at last!

To this day, Halloween is just an excuse to buy extra bags of the miniature size Reese's Peanut Butter Cups. Honestly, very few end up in the trick or treaters' bags. Eventually, they do show up-on my butt!

Occasionally, Mom would buy an item of clothing for me: funky-looking tennis shoes, jeans, or overalls- my favorite. It did not matter what I wore underneath them, not to me anyway. No one was going to check. Ribbons for my long pigtails were not necessary, she claimed. I argued that they were essential for my hair. She'd give in once or twice and let me choose the colors from the wooden spools that hung behind the counter. I'd select several colorful, bright colors, but only ended up with one very short ribbon. She said I needed to just tie the ends of my pigtails, and that didn't require a whole lot of ribbon since rubber bands did the trick.

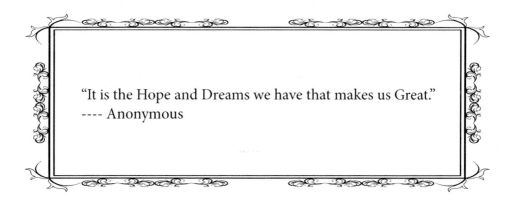

"It is the Hope and Dreams we have that makes us Great."
---- Anonymous

The Red Brick Schoolhouse

Our town's red brick schoolhouse sat just across the street from the Great Western Sugar Mill. It housed grades one through five and was made up of three floors. The first floor was the basement whose width and length equaled the size of the above floors. The basement housed the kitchen, a cafeteria/dining area, and the bathrooms. The second floor, I believe, housed grades three through five, and the third floor held the first and second grades, as well as the library.

Before stepping foot in this place, I'd never seen such shiny hardwood floors that lined in the hallway and classroom floors. The classrooms' wooden doors stood at least twenty feet tall with opaque glass panel inserts halfway up.

I spent whatever extra time I had in the library to read or complete worksheets. I even skipped playing at recess time just to catch up on assignments. If the teacher suggested some tutoring, I never declined the offer.

I remember reading my first library books: The Bobbsey Twins' Adventures. They were a series of books chronicling the adventures of the twins. The books whisked me away from everything I had known up until then. I lost myself in their great escapades. In reading the words, I traveled to New York and took a ferry to reach the Statue of Liberty, or as I called her, Freedom Lady. One of my all-time favorite stories was their expedition to hunt for real treasure buried by pirates. I read them all every year when I returned to school

By reading, I began to develop a sense of adventure and escape at a young age.

I thoroughly enjoyed all my assigned class projects. My favorite one took place every fall when we witnessed the birth of a monarch butterfly hatching out of its cocoon. In the school, science projects always involved nature. That's all we had. We collected the larvae, safely placed it in glass jars, then added slivers of grass, and a couple of dried twigs. Over time, we watched the mystery unravel, as the larvae spun its fibers around itself until completely covered in its own cocoon. The cocoon hung to one of the twigs as we waited anxiously for the miracle to happen. It evolved into a beautiful monarch butterfly which we then set it free to live out its life.

Decades later, I revisited the school grounds where my "red schoolhouse" once stood. Even though it had been demolished, the classrooms, the playground, and the smiles of everyone I ever knew remained. I felt their presence and my heart longed for those years.

I Turned Eight --- Gotta Go to School: Quite the Fashionista?

I started school in Ovid in 1960, at the age of eight, I missed out entirely the previous year. Well, that meant no more wearing jeans or overalls, now I had to dress in dresses. Talk about 'poetry in motion' as Johnny Tillotson's song says. It also takes me back to the time when I was introduced to dresses. The first day of school tomboy Emma couldn't bear being the prim and proper lady mama wanted. I was a tomboy in a dress, while secretly wearing a pair of shorts underneath my dress.

I was ordered to have my hair in pigtails, whereas before I roamed with my hair loose, windblown and knotted. No one in the family seemed to have any time to talk to me, let alone make the time to braid my hair. Remember the short ribbons I fought so hard to get? Well, I lost them somewhere in the ditches. But now, I must become this prim and proper young lady in cow-licked pigtails and razor-cut uneven bangs dressed up in a checkered dress. To become this overnight sensation I needed to undergo a transformation, no way.

Oh, let's not forget the shoes, which were black and white loafers, or were they brown and white? The tips of the shoes were longer than the rest of them. In them, my toes wiggled something awful. I called them clown shoes. Sorry Bozo, nothing personal. But, the lacey edges on my socks should have made the whole outfit the envy of the class. That didn't happen.

There wasn't any ladylikeness in me and certainly I did not care behaving as such. Mom made me wear petti pants. I still remember those. They were half-slips sewn up the middle, a split slip, pretty in pinks, pastels and white. I'd wear them under dresses and skirts. "Y ésto, que és?" ("What's this?") I asked. And she replied, "Para que no te vean los chones!" ("So they can't see your underwear!")

The idea of wearing sexy, frilly, pretty lingerie had not hit me yet. I'd pull them up to my armpits then layer on my shorts over them and off I'd go. Meanwhile, the puffiness' of the dress high up the waistline indicated some padding going on underneath. Bulky thighs were my daily norm but, eventually they became permanent.

My cow-licked pigtails and razor-cut bangs were far from fashionable. Mom slathered on some type of ointment on my hair before braiding it to keep it all in place. It had a funky smell to it. For all I knew, it could have been hemorrhoid crème. Why were there constantly several flies buzzing around my head? The tube looked identical to the tube of Parrot Crème - I think it was the same greasy gunk the boys used on their hair that seemed to drip down the back of their neck and sideburns as the day heated up.

My first dresses were all plaid: some were green, others blue, a few more I don't remember. It wasn't a matter of choice as to what "checkered" color would be the best one to compliment my skin tone. They all had a tie back and frilly ruffled hems and rick-rack trimming the ruffles. What was that all about? Ugh! My shoes were a bomb: laced up white with black or brown patches. Just call me "Patches," why don't you? Come on, now!

Mom tried hard to buy me some clothes, but remember the flour sacks made from cotton cloth. She had saved them for me, I guess for this inevitable moment of starting school. She sewed them into blouses and skirts. When I see my old school pictures flowered, checkered and print skirts and tops she made stare right back at me.

Winter began to show signs of its arrival. Thank God! I wrongly thought my dressing would change. Winterizing was not a definite plan in fashion for winter. Eventually, I got to wear pants to school during the winter months. But, they were big on me, because Mom purchased whatever pants were sold at the mercantile store at the time. And, there wasn't much of a selection, so she bought the size closest to fitting me. I could wear the same pair of pants for several days, as long as I stayed out of mud holes.

Remember I mentioned you could find EVERYTHING in Mr. Jonkovsky's store. You could. Just not in your size. She bought bulky sweaters, plaid flannel shirts for me to wear with the pants. I would have to pull the pants up all the way to my arm pits 'cause the waist was big on me. I found a picture debuting this fashion. The cuffs on the legs were rolled up several folds over my loafers. I tucked my sweater into my pants for them to stay up even though there were several layers of flannel shirts on me already. Even with all the stuffing inside of my pants, they still felt loose and the crotch hung down to my knees. As you can guess, I constantly pulled them up so they would stay on.

Mom finally took them in length and width wise, but long after I suffered. And so, this is how I began my education in the fall of 1960. I was in the first grade, fashionista and all that.

Big Chief Tablets

The month of August was a pivotal month of the year. August meant first and foremost the end to scorching and weed-pulling days in the beet fields for me since it was then that I returned to the status of student in Ovid, Colorado.

My excitement began to build around mid-month, and within a couple of days I would sign off as the youngest working "hand." Returning to school was actually my vacation, a sacred ritual in every sense of the word. I looked forward to dusting off my book satchel. I knew my satchel was always in that box of books I carried around with me from Ovid, to the Texas Pan Handle, to Edinburg.

I had worked all summer doing my share of the workload to help out. Even at that age, I knew for a fact that I had accumulated at least ninety days of back pay. I, now, had "credit" to splurge on buying my back-to-school clothing and supplies. My "rewards card" was full- it was time to redeem those points! My parents kept that money saved to buy my school supplies when the time came. How much it was in total? I was never told.

The popular "five and ten" stores in the late 1950s and 60s were equivalent to today's Sam's Club or Costco. Large families with several school age kids purchased greater quantities, while Mom and Dad made sure they stuck to the scanty list of required supplies purchasing only the minimum I needed.

Nowadays, the school supply list for today's student is over two pages long. But, we were never required to purchase fifty rolls of paper towels, twenty boxes of tissue, a gallon of hand sanitizer, and a twelve pack of disposable wipees! And, all this for just one school year! In our days, we managed to wipe our butts as best as we could with plain toilet paper. Pre-moistened towels were unheard of. We just wet the tush paper in the sink, go back into the bathroom stall, and "clean it right." That was our idea of "freshness" from "moist towels." Isn't that what we baby boomers did?

Well, back to the 60s and the list of suitable supplies was led by the incomparable Big Chief tablets, a couple of number two fat pencils, a square size thick eraser, and at least one box of Crayola's eight primary colors. The box of eight had to last me through the entire school year, but for me in reality, that translated into only five or six months of actual schooling. Other kids had boxes of sixteen, or even the popular "mother of all crayon count," the forty-eight count with a built in sharpener! What will they think of next? Sixty-four count? I simply drooled over that box, just as I had over ice cream samples. But, I played it smart. In class, I'd sit next to someone who brought that tempting array of unlimited variations of rainbow-colored crayons. I enjoyed sharing my eight with them, while they lent me their forty-eight. Even trade, huh? I thought so.

I remember the two most used crayons were red and yellow. They were the shortest with barely the wrapper sticking to a smidge of crayon. I could hardly hold them between my thumb and index finger. Most of the eight crayons were down to nubs, but I still stored them in their original box, even if it was a bit tattered, and faded. I recall the plastic pencil cases to store all the supplies, not including the tablets. It didn't fill up with just a couple of fat pencils, an eraser, and even a six inch ruler. I was on a very lean budget, so there was never a surplus. If my parents could afford an extra school item, I hung onto to it as if it were a luxury. I saved it for myself, and not for school.

The wall to wall black boards dusted in white chalk were as iconic as the Big Chief tablets, its red colored cover with an American native wearing a full headdress. They were the most popular brand of writing paper for generations of kids in the U.S., the early baby boomers. The sheet's wide- ruled bold lines guided the writer to stay within them. The broken center line perfectly aligned the letters. The final product: the entire written assignment on these sheets was neat and presentable. I first learned to write in print and then cursive in the higher grades on these light brown sheets. I suppose all of us baby boomers did. I still remember showing off my impressive "A+" to my classmates. The grade was written in red pencil on a corner of my assignment sheet. I felt I had just conquered the world because getting excellent grades was so important to me.

I don't recall using any other tablet until I was in junior high. Then, we turned our work in on white ruled paper.

The tablets were as popular then, as the IPad is now, but its cost was nowhere near the cost of an IPad. Going to the store to buy our Big Chief tablets was just as exciting as today when kids shop at Wal-Mart for the latest model of IPads. At the time, Midnight Madness sales and frantic buyers lining up outside the stores' entrances to get in on the bargains were a thing of the future. Back then, simplicity was king.

A supply of four or five of Big Chief writing tablets purchased at the beginning of the year assured me I would not run out. At ten or twenty cents apiece, I splurged a whole dollar's worth. Each tablet had about sixty pages, and for me, well, I knew I had to be conservative and not waste any sheets. I was frugal with what my parents provided because they warned me that these are all of the supplies I would have for the year when attending school in Ovid, or anywhere else.

"Friendship Gifts"

As always, the teachers in Ovid provided me with extra spelling and math worksheets to practice on while "serving time" at "Camp Caca." When we returned to Edinburg in January, I brought with me my used manuscript worksheets. I didn't throw them away. I treasured them even more because I didn't have any other paper or tablets to color or write on. So, I used the back of the sheets to draw the houses where we lived, trees, mountains, fields, and rivers.

My colorings always depicted nature and the open, unspoiled terrain, it's something I missed when living somewhere other than in Ovid. I drew the sun and the moon that were very much a part of my full day's work when we were dropped off at the fields in still pitch dark. At that time, I remember how the moon illuminated the fields, giving way to the brilliancy of the sun. And so, I made use of these recycled sheets to tearfully create my drawings of the place where I belonged. Although, they are still very much "photographed" in my mind, I wish I could have kept some of those drawings.

I folded each drawing neatly and stuffed it in brown crumpled grocery paper bags, and tied a piece of colored yarn around it. I remember where we obtained these recycled brown bags. During the month of January, upon our return to Edinburg from "Camp Caca" we rented a house at 1824 E. Harriman St (now E. University Drive). A couple by the name of Cosme and Francisca Martínez owned a vintage shop across from us, and Mom occasionally shopped there. She brought home the purchased items in these crumpled bags and I used them as gift wrapping paper. I thought they were perfect to wrap someone's gift. I recycled everything.

Once more, I created my own world, this time while living in Edinburg. When we arrived, I enrolled in an elementary school.

I took my drawings, my "friendship gifts" to school. I had nothing else to offer kids to win their friendship during my short stay. Even though I was timid, I wanted somebody as my comrade. I wasn't totally stiff and unfriendly, but if I could persuade one or two, then perhaps we'd be buddies for the times my family lived in Edinburg.

I was lonely and I desperately missed my true friends in Ovid. But the girls in Edinburg looked at me as if I were strange because there were no store bought gifts inside the bags when they opened them. They expected something of value, but the disappointed look on their faces is what I recall. My drawings colored on the backs of my math or spelling work sheets did not impress them. I walked away feeling dejected and ridiculed by their responses. It made the three months living in Edinburg just as desolate and "cold" as the dreaded winter months at "Camp Caca" in the Texas Pan Handle.

Looking back over the years, I realized it was their loss for not accepting me. I gave them something special of myself. Perhaps, they felt they didn't deserve it, or worse yet they failed to "see" the value of the gift, my friendship. I preferred this reason rather than the idea that I didn't merit their companionship.

Luckily, my attempts would not be a total loss. After a couple of years, the camaraderie of three classmates lessened the severity of my despondency that had plagued me for years. A lonely decade began, but I would "win over" a few new friends in Edinburg.

School, or the Fields - In Ovid

I rode the school bus, as it made its punctual stop about seven in the morning, right behind the yellow house. I would cross the canal via a narrow wooden bridge to get to the bus stop.

My first day of school is still a bit of a blur. From the time I stepped onto the bus, until I arrived at the school grounds and made my way to the principal's office, I blanked out.

Years of being left out in the fields, abandoned, and traumatized, I figured this would be the same or worse. I was wrong. Thankfully, school turned out a completely different experience, a pleasant one. I was far removed from the trauma and pain I suffered through the first three years. I had experienced only the labor camps up until then. I think the only reason I was put in school was because of some labor laws that protected kids from working when they should have been in school. Otherwise, my parents would not have enrolled me in school on their own. But, it was Mr. Tom Kobayashi who strongly "advised" them to do so.

I believe the teacher welcomed me in that first day. I think her name was Mrs. Bertha Spreick. Now that I think of it, was she my second grade teacher, too? Anyhow, she asked me my name—that I understood. I shyly whispered, "Emma." She walked me over to a desk, in the front of the classroom, near her. I think the class shouted "Hello" because they all sounded friendly. Meanwhile, I am terrified! Now I'm in a room full of people I don't know. People scared me, regardless of their size. I was used to me—"UNO, NO MAS!" ("ONE, NO MORE!") As I recall, the rest is a blur. I arrived home that afternoon. I remember that. But, no one was home.

I knew there were several other families with children, living in surrounding areas, in neighboring towns because I recall seeing them with school-aged children in town and in Julesburg. They had traveled in the caravan of trucks at the same time we were recruited. However, it's possible they may have stayed at home if someone took care of them. Meanwhile, they may have been working in the fields, for all I know. As far as kids enrolled in school, there were probably two or three others older than me.

It didn't take long to adjust to school. I started to make friends, though we communicated in different languages at first, but we understood each other. I don't think we used sign language, because friendship is a universal language entirely of its own.

Many of the kids in class volunteered to "tutor" me during class. Any one of them would pull up a chair next to me to work the assignment together. I remember getting the giggles every time someone sat next to me, particularly if it was a boy, however the boys didn't shy away from me. They helped me enunciate words, while I read along with them. At times, the teacher called on me for an answer. Surprisingly, I knew the answer and I'd blurt it out. My correct response was met with cheers of approval from the kids because I had answered it. There's nothing better than supportive peers.

Although the entire class befriended me, four students would turn out special friends through the coming years: they were Jody Lauer, Jane Taylor, April Lechman and Raymond Schneider.

My third grade teacher was Mrs. Joan Brownell. I remember how she encouraged me and how she made time for me in between subjects. I didn't mind staying in during recess to get her tutoring. Mrs. Melba Snyder, the fourth grade teacher, was the sweetest soul, she styled her gray hair pulled back in a bun. Mrs. Snyder and Mrs. Brownell looked after me, gave me written assignments, used textbooks, whatever they could find for me to take while I was away.

I can't say enough about these teachers. Their lifework was teaching the three "Rs" (Reading, wRiting, and aRithmetic), more importantly, their compassion went beyond supportive, it was noble, genuine. What I received from them is a genuinely heart-felt gift which indebted me to them forever for helping to build the life I have now.

If there was one favorite time of the day at school, I have to say it was lunch period. I loved the cafeteria food. The entrees were so diverse. I loved my daily tacos, but I experienced "American" food, such as casseroles, shredded pork and beans, and a delightful fruit salad concoction. I looked forward to my favorite: Sloppy Joes, served piled high with the meat – sauce fillings, oozing out the sides of the buns. It was a mess to eat, but so delicious. I'd woof it down in no time. With certainty, the evidence of stains on my "checkered" dress would upset Mom.

I felt that I truly belonged in Ovid's schools. There was no difference because of my last name or because I spoke Spanish. My family spoke Spanish all the time at home. That was their only language, with the exception of a few critical English words spoken to get by. I had no trouble learning English or speaking English. I learned at the same pace as the Anglo kids, because I was taught right along with them.

If I needed something repeated, it was repeated once, and then I'd quickly catch on. When pointed to an object, the teacher would pronounce it in English, and I repeated it back to her. Several times of repetition about an object or a word sunk in for me. It was the easiest way I was taught. I welcomed the extra help offered to me between subjects, or during recess, at times. No ESL there! English was the primary and only language taught and spoken, and I soaked it up like a sponge. Perseverance pre-

Mr. Tom Kobayashi.....thank you!

vailed.

I attended school April and May then worked the summer months in the fields, most of the time, though I did get a break now and then to keep up with my reading. I took books to the fields to read. In August, I started the new school year through October, even through November, depending on the number of fields harvested. We then left after the beet harvest for the Texas Pan Handle to work the cotton gins.

The teachers in Ovid gave me assignments and reading materials to work on, as well as outdated reading or math books to take with me so I wouldn't fall behind when I returned in April. I can't remember any other place where teachers cared as much about me and about my education. I am deeply, deeply grateful to them that they went out of their way and gave me reading books

My first report card in Ovid's Schools – 1960. I had all As and Bs.

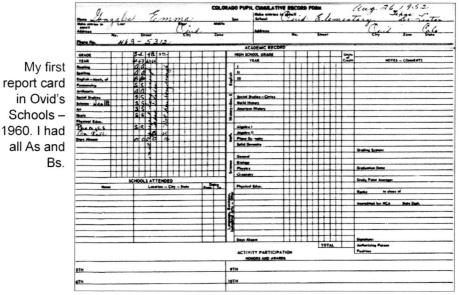

and workbooks to take with me. Their generosity and goodness in their hearts fueled my desire to envision the grandness of our universe. That says it all, doesn't it?

As I mentioned earlier, my parents would not have enrolled me in school if it hadn't been for Mr. Kobayashi's concern that I was working the fields instead of being in school. He told them that I needed my education. He altered my path from field labor forever.

Once I enrolled in Ovid's schools, I chose education and I directed my own path for a better life.

I owe him immensely. I was at the right place at the right time in my life, regardless, of how I arrived there. It was fate.

Fifty plus years later, as an adult, I returned to visit Ovid. Although my childhood friends moved away, and one of them, Jane Taylor passed away, I reunited with Jody Lauer Jimenez, Raymond Schneider, and my first best friend, Patty Schneider, to thank them for their true friendship through the years. I hold them dearly in my heart. I also stopped in to see Mrs. Kiyo Kobayashi, Mr. Tom Kobayashi's widow to thank her. It was important for her to know how Mr. Kobayashi's considerate actions altered the rest of my life, and how eternally grateful I am to him. While there, I visited their "white house," the first place I really called home.

Mrs. Kiyo Kobayashi and daughter Donna Miller to my left; at their farm during my visit to Ovid in 2013.

Every year when we left Ovid to work elsewhere, I attended different schools depending where we were taken, two months at a time at three different locations within the year or no schooling at all in others. Regardless of where I was dragged, school or no school, I knew I had a great supportive team back home, in Ovid.

Show Me *Some* Money

The first three years were the most difficult ones for the family, simply because we were at the mercy of the dim-witted, idiot foreman who transported us to and from Ovid. Although it was a yearly, grueling trip to and from, I looked forward only to the fume-choking adventure that got us to Ovid. I could have cared less about the other pit stop made in the Texas Pan Handle.

I knew Dad realized what he was facing. I heard him complain and cuss even more than the previous two years. These "pioneers" were burned out, at least that's what I sensed from overhearing conversations between Dad and what was left of his family's stock pile of workers. Perhaps he felt there was no turning back, at least not for him. So, he pushed on, with hope.

Earnings were minimal from all those months of hard labor in Ovid, but I remember him saying it paid a lot better than in Texas. Dad explained that we were paid on the number of rows thinned and weeded. It must have been pennies/cents on the dollar.

I know that they were paid in installments, and not often. Pay depended on the acreage cleared. We were able to buy clothing, if needed, and we could charge our groceries. The boys received some allowance to buy whatever they needed for work on some occasions.

On these days, I put my hand out just to see if something would drop into it. Consequently, I might have been given a dime, a couple of nickels, or even a whole quarter. But, I don't remember that happening too many times.

Nevertheless, desperate times called for desperate measures. I perfected my own compensation scheme unbeknown to the rest of the world. Whenever the boys changed jeans and left the dirty ones lying around by the beds or on the floor I went through them to see if something jingled in the pockets. A penny or two would fall out. If I were lucky the find would be multiplied by four pairs of pants. I raked it in, at times, finding six or eight cents. I was a pickpocket in the making. I hid my findings behind the outhouse in a coffee can and piled on sticks or rocks to keep my treasure hidden. I figured no one would go behind the stench looking for buried treasure, my treasure. It took me weeks to get a substantial amount of loose change.

I recall a time when we went to the mercantile for supplies and groceries taking my pennies with me. As far as I could count, at the time, I'd say I had about fifteen cents. I took out the pennies from my pants pocket and laid them on the counter. The owner, Mr. Jonkovsky came over, and somehow we communicated. I timidly requested "dulce" ("candy"). I pointed to a Reese's Peanut Butter Cup. The bright orange wrapper caught my eye. I shoved the entire candy into my mouth. I can still taste the decadent melted chocolate as the peanut butter stuck to the roof of my mouth, I remember frantically using my tongue to shove it down my throat to keep from choking. Back then, only one cup was sold per package, so I don't know how many pennies he took for the price of the candy, but he kept most of them. I think he gave me back three pennies. So, I'm thinking they must have cost five or eight cents each. My math does not add up.

I knew then I was on to something big. Every time I found precious pennies, I ran to back of the outhouse and put them in my coffee can. Over time, I became richer, things improved, and I graduated up from just buying peanut butter cups, even though they were always my favorites.

Once a month we were taken to the next town over called Julesburg. There was a variety of stores, a "five and ten," a couple soda shops, and some retail shops. I do not recall buying anything at the retail shops opting to window shopped instead. I hung out at the five and ten cent store (a store similar to The Dollar Tree nowadays) admiring the costume jewelry. It was beautiful and consisted of earrings, bracelets, necklaces made out of crystal beads, and simulated pearl strands.

The pearls caught my eye because they had a creaminess, a satin smooth feel, an elegance about them, definitely regal. I was hooked on them even though they were not real. I bought a strand and I'd wear it every day to the field -- along with two or three rings of dirt around my neck, but Hey! I was into my own fashion mode and in my own world.

I modeled my fashionable pearls to my mousy audience - I received great reviews from them, really! I found a second or third grade school photo in which I am wearing my elegant pearl necklace.

"Nights of a Thousand Eyes"

The Cortez farm house.

1961 brought change. We ended up living in a different location, not far from the Kobayashi places, on the next road just south, with less family members. The two oldest half -brothers chose not to make the trip, and my half-sister had eloped the previous winter, so we were down to five.

A farmer by the name of Bruno Cortez and his son, Richard lent us a place near their farm, and I enrolled in school for the typical two months of April and May. The house was a frame bungalow with two bed-

The mystical cherry trees still sway behind me.

rooms and, of course, an outhouse. There was a cherry tree orchard right next to the house that became my getaway.

The aroma of homemade tortillas still lingers.

I became friends with a little girl by the name of Patricia Schneider, "Patty," as we came to call her. Jerry and Ronnie were her older brothers. Her parents, Jake and Mary Schneider, farmed beets and lived directly across the road from us. I remember their gray stucco house was surrounded by giant cottonwood trees and an irrigation canal crossing by the front entrance to their farm. Their farm had a huge barn with the weather vane whirling with the wind. A rustic bunkhouse was found across it, which eventually would house us for the next four seasons.

I can still hear the rustling of the wind-blown leaves in the giant cottonwoods.

Patty and I were inseparable. Our two-year difference in age didn't matter to us. I saw her as a younger sister, and any free time I had, we'd be together. She'd converse with us as much as she could. I'd teach her some important Spanish words, for example: "tortillas," "frijoles," and "mi casa." That's all I thought she really needed to know.

When she came over to the house, she smelled the appetizing aromas in the

Patty Schneider
– my first playmate and friend.

kitchen. Just as we were rolling out the tortillas, she grabbed a puffy one coming off the griddle. We pulled out the sticks of but-

The white door led to my room.

ter from the fridge and we'd cut up chunks of and smear them into the tortilla. The butter melted immediately. We'd roll them up into burrito with gobs of butter. We didn't care that it dripped all over us. And, then we devoured the refried bean tacos! "Girl, what you talking about!" We had a feast every day. I think these are the best memories we shared and remembered.

She enjoyed hanging around us, speaking some Spanish, and eating Mexican food. We loved her as if she were one of us. As I said earlier, I saw her as my younger sister. She was very comfortable with us and her parents trusted us.

After feasting on freshly made tortillas and bean tacos, or "carne guisada,"(stewed meat in Mexican spices and gravy) she stayed over late into the evenings at our place listening to the radio in the truck. We'd open the doors, roll down the windows. We had no other entertainment except listening to music every night to KOMA, from Oklahoma City.

We'd lie on the truck's hood and stargaze for hours, as Bobby Vinton's song "She Wore Blue Velvet" whisked us off on a magic carpet ride into the Milky Way.

We didn't know about constellations, but we made out star patterns and tried connecting the dots/stars. We had a plethora of star-connecting wonders to outlast our lives, I suppose. We challenged each other to connect the most visible ones, including the Big Dipper: we thought it looked like a deep spoon, a ladle. I could relate to that one because we had one in our water containers.

The endless chatter, the giggling and outbursts of laughter echoed late into the night. When we retired, we knew the star-lit celestial spheres will return tomorrow night and we'll be right back where we'd left off the night before.

We don't hear Mary calling out to Patty. "Patty"! "Patty"! Mary is at the edge of the road. So, Dad and I would walk her to the other side of the road to get her home.

I hope that she remembers the wonderful memories of us as I do of her.

She learned Spanish quickly. She called Mom "Chabela" for Chavela. And, her favorite question for Mom was "Can she, Chabela, can Emma go to my house, or can she go with us?" Wherever that may be: to her house, to the store, etc., they'd take me along if I wasn't out in the fields.

One time, Jake took Mary, Patty, and me to a car dealership to bring home their new car. It was a rose-mauve color, four-door Buick with lots of shiny chrome all around it. I think it had air conditioning, too. I had never been in a car, let alone in a brand new one. It smelled so wonderful and clean on the inside, I wanted to take my shoes off before climbing in.

We took Patty into town with us on Saturdays for our weekly shopping trips. We'd go to Mr. Jonkovsky's store first. There wasn't one Saturday, I don't think, and that we didn't get Reese's Peanut Butter Cups and malted ice cream in cups. I remember using tiny wooden spoons to scoop the frozen delight. We'd go through five or six spoons because they'd crack - we had to make sure we didn't accidentally swallow wooden pieces. Our last stop of decadence was the corner drugstore for a flavored soda topped with scoops of vanilla ice cream, thick chocolate malt, or a milk shake. We never tired of eating ice cream any given day.

By the second grade, I'd made friends with practically everyone in the class, including Patty's cousins Raymond, Suzie, and Bobby who lived across the corn fields and alfalfa fields just a short distance from her farm. A narrow wandering road along the edge of the fields led to their cousins' house, and another Schneider family--John Schneider, Jake's brother. Raymond was in my class, and Suzie, I think she was Patty's age, with Bobby a couple years older.

Anyway, we'd hang around together playing in the corn fields or in the irrigation ditches. Even now, I can remember the smell of the husks and the corn silk strands as we stripped them off the cob. Eating fresh hot corn smothered in butter was a special summer treat. Real butter just made everything taste lip-smacking delicious, from the flour tortillas to freshly harvested, cooked corn on the cob.

With our creativity and imagination we invented fun projects.

We made rafts from just about any material we could get our hands on. Excitedly, we began our much anticipated "canal rafting" adventures, as we tried to sail down the irrigation canals when the pump houses were in use. Most of the time, it was the pump house right next to Patty's house that pumped with the greatest force to thrust the raft the furthest distance down the canal. We got the greatest thrills when we tried to sail as far as the water current pushed us. This kind of entertainment was the "Schlitterbahn" of our time. Our short lived "cruise" ended when the raft came tumbling apart. Then, we quickly scrambled to try to piece it together again- we were on a "mission," determined to beat the frigid, "wild rapids."

The ice-cold water pumped from underground rivers froze our butts, but what a ride! We were left shivering in our shorts for a while, as the sun's warmth thawed us out.

We rode bikes. Patty lent me her old squeaky, beat-up one, while she rode her new shiny, pink bike. It had all the pretty streamers hanging off the handlebars, and a cute basket attached to the bar handle. We rode along the dirt road from her house straight up to the top of the hill where Jane and Debbie Taylor lived in their two story white house. Most of the time we walked alongside the bikes, trying to reach the top, but then we coasted down doing a hundred miles an hour.

I didn't mind so much working the fields now because I had real friends to come home to, the non-mousy kind. At least, now I ended each day with fun and laughter.

In spite of all the great fun we had, there was a serious incident that occurred and it was all my doing. Several of the kids, including myself, had trapped some spiders in Jake's barn and put them in a glass jar. We drilled holes in the lid to let in air. Anyhow, we took the spiders to class the next day for "show and tell." That afternoon on our way home on the bus, we let them out of the jar. Kids began screaming and standing on the bus seats, as the spiders crawled their way down the center aisle of the bus. Mr. Ray Burgess, our bus driver, bless his soul, pulled over the bus. He walked right up to the spiders and stomped on them! Poor spiders never saw that coming. I don't recall anyone of us getting into trouble. I think we explained the lids came off because they were loose.

I find myself reminiscing about an era of simplicity, a time of rooted friendships, laughter, and innocence. This is when I lived the best years of my childhood. Those majestic times are chiseled in my mind, untouched over the years. Honestly, I think that the ice-cold water just "froze" instantly those whimsical memories. Someday, I will tell my grandchildren about those magical years, the memories I have treasured all of my life, and of the wonderful people who made them possible

Hot Cherries!

A great summer ended as August signaled the time for scavenging cherries on the Cortez farm. We played long enough in that orchard. We sat under the trees, passing the time away, drinking some Kool Aid or sodas, maybe even munching on chips, cookies, whatever we could get. We ran out of stories to tell. We had waited patiently all summer to treat ourselves to the delectable fruit. It would be a first for me. I didn't know how they tasted, but Patty's description of the sweet and tasty treat built up my anticipation.

We were impatient to indulge in the sweet tartness of this bright, red forbidden fruit in the trees. It was forbidden to eat when the cherries that were somewhat green or hot from the day's heat.

Patty, myself, and I believe Suzie, decided to eat some. We were supposed to chill them for a while before eating them, but we jumped into eating them right off the tree. And, I don't mean just a couple of them. How can I put this mildly? After we had eaten them, our stomachs began to growl simultaneously. We looked at each other as we scurried out of the orchard while grabbing our stomachs! Patty and Suzie, bless her heart, rushed towards Patty's house and I raced to my outhouse. I think we all made it without incident. The moral of this short excerpt: make sure the cherries are ripe and chilled. Otherwise, you'll be whistling "Dixie" for a spell.

My Arrowheads

We returned to the Cortez farm for a second and final year. Besides playing with Patty in the evenings, I hunted arrow heads during the long daytime hours. My source of entertainment for the most part was to roam the fields while my family worked. Once I finished my share of hoeing, I took off. I got out of the ditch to stretch my legs a bit. I'd walk away from the main field, looking for pretty rocks and arrowheads along the irrigation ditches to the edge of the road, and sometimes along the South Platte River bank.

That summer, I filled up a couple of coffee cans with my artifacts, my go-to collection. I found the rocks and arrowheads in the world I wandered. Native Americans had roamed that territory in earlier days. I revered their free, spirited nature. Often, their numerous presences paralleled mine. Thus, my finding of their arrowheads and other relics were priceless to me.

Right next to the bungalow that we lived in, on the east side, was a run-down shack, an open garage with a dirt floor. I left my collection in the shack the first year we lived there. When we returned the second year, I filled up a third can. Unfortunately, when we left after the harvest, my parents did not let me take my collection. They insisted we had overloaded the truck. It was either my box of reading material and books or the rocks. I had worked hard to accumulate what was in those cans. I had walked countless miles to find them, and they denied me such a simple request. I couldn't understand them. I remember I had a "spew" with them, lots of anger and several curse words that erupted out of me. I can't remember specifically the words I blurted, but they were not pleasant ones. I had to choose. But, I had no real choice, the books won. I took my books with me, but tearfully left my collection hidden in a corner of that shack. I prayed no one would ever find them. I vowed that someday I would come back for them.

The following year, we came to live on Patty's farm. When we arrived, I immediately ran to the shack looking for them. My treasures were gone! There weren't any people living there when we arrived, but that doesn't mean someone else hadn't gone in there and taken them. Whoever it was, they acquired a precious treasure that had taken me two long, hot summers to find for myself.

I held so many grudges against my folks. I accumulated grudges throughout the years on a variety of issues affecting me. I was a helpless kid with no say. I had no face in that one - sided family. It was nothing to them, but to me, it was outrageous and unfair.

The Whipping

We lived on the Cortez farm, and then moved to Jake's place. Regardless of where we lived in Ovid, I was surrounded by farmers' kids who befriended me. The sister team of Jane and Debbie Taylor always dropped by my place on their way to visit their grandparents, Carl and Eleanor Williams. Their farm was visible, a distance of just a couple of blocks from Patty's place on County Road 34, however, Patty and her cousins were closer to me.

County Road 34 was a busy farm road, upgraded to a "highway" not only for farm trucks and machinery traveling on it, but also for kids riding bicycles and tricycles during the summer months. Amongst the "wild bunch of bikers" were Patty, Raymond, Suzie, and the Taylor girls, even the younger Taylor siblings, as well as Raymond's younger brothers. I wheeled on a bike borrowed from Patty. I didn't care if it was beat up as long as it wheeled me around and I didn't get left behind.

Keeping track of time was not a priority for the fun bunch during the summer months. One summer day, Jane and Debbie came by and we hooked up with Patty, Suzie, and Raymond. We all went over to the Williams' place. It was a Saturday because we played in the cornfields for most of the day, so that means I was not working out in the fields. As for me, my Saturdays brought a bit of fun, a much needed break.

The Williams were generous and loving grandparents who provided sandwiches, Kool Aid, and cookies as snacks for all of us. They fed a large group of "adopted" grandkids. That day we barricaded ourselves within the green acres as we cleared a narrow patch within the cornfield for all of us to play in. The girls pretended to be up in the castle of princesses, hidden behind the cornfield "walls" that protected us from witches. I don't think Raymond was in on this one, if he had been, he would have been our designated knight in shining armor to protect us beauties.

As our food supplies dwindled, we knew we had to return to the real world outside our "fortress" of giant shielding corn stalks to replenish our supplies. And, so we did.

As we came out of the field, my mother arrived, she was the Wicked Witch of the West. She walked to the farm's entrance with a look on her face that scared every living gnat out of that cornfield. I shook shitless in my shoes! We stood watching her as she approached us. No one moved. I spotted in her hand what appeared as twigs or branches. I knew I was dead meat. You can surmise what happened next.

She grabbed me by the arm and pulled me with her. She kept asking me where I had been, and why I hadn't come home. As we crossed onto the road, she began whipping me with the twigs, striking my legs and calves, then moving up to the buttocks. For the next two blocks or so, she whipped, then talked some more. She alternated the whipping with the same conversation over and over. I didn't have an excuse that she would believe for my absence from home. Nothing I explained to her would have made a difference to stop the beating- she pelted me with the twigs, in rhythm to every cry I let out.

My legs burned, God, did they burn! To this day, I remember the feverish sting as she whacked my thighs and buttocks. I squirmed around a bit trying to avoid the thrash as her hand came down on me, but as if she were a "pro boxer," she landed more "punches" on my protruding "plump tush" than on my legs. I felt it more painfully there than on my boney calves. It took something awful to calm down that area. I'm sure the thrashes were more evident on my rump than on my legs. I guess a wide, magnifying mirror would have revealed a more serious outcome.

All that mattered to me was that I had escaped to a fantasy world for a while, but she brought me right back to reality really quickly with the thrashing. No wonder I spent so much time in my "castle in the sky." It was hard to keep it together for myself and not go off on the negatives. I'd hoped for the best, but then my "burning" ass kept reminding me otherwise.

Worse than the whipping, I truly hated the lifestyle we lived every day, year after year....if only we'd stay put in Ovid.

Needless to say, she grounded me for, I don't recall how long. Patty would come knocking at our door looking for me to play with her, but Mother turned her away.

Twist Some Time Away...

Life was a bit more bearable after having lived through the first five years as a migrant. Besides my furry, mouse buddies, Patty and friends, I discovered a new entertainment. Thank God for Rock and Roll music! I listened to the radio in the truck for a few minutes each day, making sure the battery wouldn't die off.

Too many times, I had seen the boys turn the key in the ignition to the left. Hello, KOMA, Oklahoma City! KOMA ruled. Chubby Checker never sounded so electrifying, and I'd twist away some of the time with him.

Out in the boonies, alone with Nature, there was nothing else in sight. Just entertaining myself once my folks disappeared into oblivion, (the other side of the field) they couldn't hear if I turned up that sucker loudly. So, I turned up the volume the max in the truck.

We were a threesome: nature, me, and, Chubby Checker twisting away by the ditch while I pulverized chunks of dried mud. I could grind those chunks of dirt to fine dust, marking my spot where I had done some serious twisting that day. If I twisted or stomped, I didn't know the difference. My legs moved to the rhythm of their own, sending the beat to my feet.

Most of the time, the "oldies" were just enough to get me through the day. They became the essence of me, the rhythm in my heart. I am those songs and the songs are me.

I'd climb back into the ditch after turning off the truck's radio and chill a while. I still had my old tarp put up all the time. It didn't matter that now we had a vehicle that I could stay inside. I preferred to stay under my tent, it was my "safe haven" as in past years, like Linus and his blankee. We spent some incredible, and memorable moments together, and I had my loyal friends pop out of nowhere, Papo, Lulu, Lala and others. "We'd be peas in a pod." It was a unique doing, my naughty playfulness.

Come nighttime, I stargazed while I listened to music from the truck's speakers. It was my nightly sacred ritual. What else was there to do? Some of the songs always had a message or command: "Don't cry," "Stand by me," "Hey! Mr. Sandman, bring me a dream."

The catchy song, "Limbo Rock" was instructional too. It kept repeating "how low can you go?" Well, that just sounded silly to me. To go "how low" regarding what? Obviously, it was a light hearted rhythm, so I figured it's something fun related. Without exactly knowing how to dance to this particular beat, I figured it out myself. The male singer's baritone voice deepened after each repeat of "how LOW can you go." He sounded as though

These Grand Ladies of the Plains are the vestiges of my past.
Their beacons of light renew the soul of this migrant child.

The Kobayashi houses on County Rd. 36.

The Schneider bunkhouse and the Cortez farm house on County Rd. 34.

he himself was sinking lower and lower. So, I put two beat-up wooden chairs side by side, a few feet apart. I placed a broomstick between the chairs.

Aha! I had another fun project in the making. I began to squat underneath the broom stick, the baritone's voice clearly guiding me, as I hopped my way under it, lowering my head to miss the broomstick. An acrobat in the making! No sooner had I done my "hopping" under the broom a few times, then I hear another command. This time, however, not from the blaring of the truck speakers but rather an ominous tone of terror: "Emma, traeme la escoba!" ("Emma, bring me the broom!") It was clearly my mother commanding me to bring her "the limbo bar," along with my hopping a** to sweep the floors.

The chairs remained in the same location outside the back door. I knew that sometime, in the very near future, I would return to my nightly acrobatics. A broom would always be in the house. It served multi-purposes for both "fun/functional."

Weekends! Fun Times

Three years later, we still didn't have any electronics, not a radio or television set. During the weeknights, we had KOMA blasting away out of the speakers in the truck. However, on Saturday nights Patty would invite me over to her house to watch the Ed Sullivan show on TV.

Who can forget the Beatles when they appeared? It was the first time ever I saw them. Patty and I decided which of the four was the cutest. We both fell in love with Paul.

Mary would make a huge bowl of popcorn and hand out plastic bowls to Jake, Jerry, Ronnie and us, and we'd fill them up with piping hot buttery popcorn. Pepsi Cola "soda pop" ruled as our Saturday night beverage. I remember the glass bottles with the red and blue insignia on it, and there was only one true way to drink it: use a colorful straw. We would choose our favorite colors.

Afterwards, Patty and I helped Mary clean-up for the night and do the dishes. I remember the fresh scent of the dish detergent brand called "Joy" she used for dish washing. I recall the suds overflowing from the sink. We must have poured half of the bottle in at one time.

Years later, when I shopped with Mom, I preferred that dish detergent and put it in the shopping cart. When I washed dishes it reminded me so much of Mary. Its scent instantly took me back to their house. I remember shedding a tear or two. Although fifteen hundred miles separated us, they were still in my heart.

Since we had a vehicle of our own now, we went to drive-in movies on Friday nights in neighboring Julesburg. We piled into the back of the pickup (with Patty too), and headed into Julesburg. I remember watching Disney movies with Haley Mills, "In Search of the Castaways," "The Shaggy Dog," Alfred Hitchcock's "The Birds." Dad's favorites were John Wayne's westerns.

The kids would run to the playground with the swings and merry-go rounds to watch the movie. We only ate popcorn and a soda because the A & W Drive-In was just downtown. It was the best way to finish off the night with piled-high cheeseburgers, fries, and tall frosty mugs of root beer floats topped with rich, creamy vanilla ice cream.

We waited for the best part of the night. We stayed in the truck to order our food. The waitresses promptly brought our orders. I can taste that frosty mug of root beer as I write about it. I dipped my straw into the triple scoop, high mounds of vanilla ice cream. I could never refrain from sipping the frosty ice-cold mesh of root beer and melted cream. Forget the straw. I took a couple of gigantic swallows. Oh, Heavenly Mother, brain freeze! A few brain cells got preserved in cryogenics, but in my case, the abuse resulted in permanent obliteration.

Rock and Roll music from all the current top artists including the do-wops groups, teen idols, and girl groups of the sixties was piped outside as well as inside.

I can almost hear my all-time favorite, Frankie Lymon's song "Little Bitty Pretty One," a finger snapping, and a humdinger of a great song. Rock and Roll music thrived during that era of innocence. No wonder they were called "Happy Days."

Third Verse, More of the Curse!

In the following two years, 1960 and 1961, we returned to Midway-Lubbock, Texas, the land of Buddy Holly. I recall the boys talking about him, how he died in a plane crash, but certainly not his music. "Peggy Sue" was a favorite played on KOMA.

The days of traveling in "Bondo" were over. Hallelujah! Nonetheless, we're back residing in that "infamous camp." This time we traveled in our truck, and KOMA reigns again. We'd listen to its oldies format of rock and roll music all the way from Ovid to Lubbock, and further.

At least once a week, I could mellow out listening to KOMA in the truck on our way to town for the weekly shopping. I didn't have access to the truck, hardly ever saw it parked out front. One of the boys drove it to work. Therefore, one day out of the week to listen to KOMA was a festival on a sunny day.

More importantly, I had already started school in Ovid, Colorado. This meant my education was back on track. Even though I was not enrolled in the Pan Handle schools, for three months I kept busy working on assignments that the teachers in Ovid had given me. I read all the time, sometimes reading the same books repeatedly. I'd even hauled a box of outdated or unused subject books, such as science, math, and geography to review.

Time passed so quickly locked up inside the barrack. It was my choice not to venture outside too much. I feared coming in contact with any kids my age. Memories of that lice infestation traumatized me for a long time.

While at the camp, I looked forward to a mild sunny day when I could sit by the doorstep to read. Wooden ramps were placed right outside the door entrance for stable footing, occasionally, they served as mini benches to sit on. Oh, how I loved the sun's radiating warmth to sooth my face, like Calgon "taking me away" to a lush tropical island. After a while, I'd open my eyes, having "floated" for a while. No one could touch me while in my escapes. I'd "float" regardless of where I really was.

I would have preferred to have been left behind, if my family didn't care to check if I was in the back of the truck. Otherwise, I couldn't stand the sights around me, the barren fields, dust whirling across them, and grave yards of decaying, rusting trucks and cars abandoned and scattered throughout the desolate outlying areas of the barracks. Several beat up cars had been dumped not far from our front door. On sunny days I remember watching dirty, raggedy-looking kids playing in them, scurrying in and out of the carcasses, gutted out and stripped of everything. This was their playground.

I closed my eyes and envisioned the trees, plants, mountains, blooming flowers, faraway lands. Whatever I read about in books would "take me away" to a distant place and time.

As I reflect back, wastefulness and decay swamped my surroundings, as if ravaged by a past war and sealed off in a time capsule. Post-apocalyptic.

It's My Party at "Camp Caca:" 1961

Sometimes, amid the squalor, a blessing would come, but then also the most unexpected shit could happen at any given moment. Sometimes, simultaneously. We'd finished the harvest earlier than most years this time around, so it stands to reason, we'd drive to the Pan Handle earlier.

Out of nowhere, Mom threw a birthday party for me for my 9th birthday. Go figure. I don't know what to say about it other than being caught completely by surprise! I had already celebrated my birthday in Colorado, without a party. I took candy to share with the class.

OCT 61

"Possessed" walking doll.
– Chuckee's great-grandmother!

What could have triggered this party idea? I think she'd been standing by that burner too long, too many years, and she just short circuited, or maybe she wanted me to have friends. Anyhow, what do I do, now? I certain-

Lice committee and guests attend grand gala!

ly wasn't a party animal in the camp. Surprisingly, she managed to round up a few kids. God knows who, I had no friends there.

The Lice Committee undoubtedly attended. I remembered some of the faces from a couple years back. Someone shouted the word "party" and a bunch of kids showed up. Not one of them was an acquaintance, let alone, a friend.

I got a piñata, a pointy party hat, a new dress, combed hair, and lacy socks. I was all gussied up for my party.

The pictures taken that day tell so much more of those

OCT 61

The piñata's demise.

times. Mother moved me to the front of our rat hole of a barrack, number twenty-eight, for a photo-op. The scenery behind
me is that of gray barracks against a gray sky. The wooden door
and window are perfectly showcased behind me. The two old,
abandoned vehicles, a beat-up pickup truck and a wrecked car
grace the entrance to our neighboring barracks. They are a stark

contrast to the party décor.

In the first picture, I stand alone holding my birthday present: a giant walking doll. She holds a woven basket in her cold, plastic hand. A pointy birthday hat muddles her perfectly curled fake blond hair. Her pinafore fits flawlessly on her. My purple dress that had gathered puffy, sleeves and lacey edges is too tight for me. I itched 'til kingdom came. Unimpressed with the situation at hand, I failed to smile for the picture, not a hint of a smirk. My facial expression is that of a sour puss, looking down at the barren compacted ground.

A second photo reveals the "guests:" the who's who of the camp. I have no idea who they are. Twelve girls, ages between four and probably twelve take center stage in front of me, smiling at the camera. I tower above them. They dressed in their Sunday best dresses, petticoats, and lacy pinafores, they cast color against the gray barracks' background. The pointy hats tip in all directions. Everyone has her own style of wearing the party hats: plastered on their foreheads, some covering their ears, others cover their "bad dos" with all the corralling pesky critters roaming their scalps, no doubt.

I frown and continue to stare at the dirt.

This last photo depicts the highlights of that afternoon. The camera caught me from the back. My petticoat hung out and was torn. Something is attached to a cable or rope rising with the wind. I have a piñata, Hey, Hey! As the honoree, I am blind folded, and given a huge "mother stick" with which to strike it, in hopes of busting its guts which undoubtedly are filled with treats. Frustrated at my misses, I keep swinging at the damned piñata with the stick, but I can't touch it. It's flying off in the hurricane- strength winds. Ultimately, my frustration and anger drain the last ounce of patience in me. I yank the blind fold off and cast it to the dissipating winds. Only then, could I actually see the piñata to beat the crap out of it – as miniature candies and treats scattered to the wind.

Billowing white clouds miraculously appeared against the deep azure skies. I couldn't remember ever seeing such resplendent, intense blue heavens, certainly not at this forsaken camp. I believe the angels cued the sun shining its brilliance on my special day overwhelming that gray afternoon. It rendered its glorious color of brightness and presence as my special gift. I feel its warmth, as if wishing me a happy day, so to speak. It deserves a standing ovation. These special signs from God gave me reassurance of His looking out for me.

I've Got the Whole World...

I believe it was 1962 when I discovered S&H stamps issued at Piggy Wiggly or Safeway grocery chain stores. I can't recall which one it was. The stamps were issued with the purchase of groceries depending on the amount spent. These stamps would be pasted into a booklet, filling it entirely, and then the booklets could be redeemed for promotional items offered by the store such as dishes, pots and pans, and even books.

Mom collected the stamps but she didn't redeem them for the fancy glass dinner plates, cups, saucers, sugar bowls, plates, and dinner glasses. In our gypsy life, dented aluminum cookware traveled better than china without breaking and dents were okay and nothing leaked from them. These dishes were too fancy to even look at.

So, she gave me the booklets, and I chose to redeem them for books. I was in book heaven when I glimpsed at the types of books offered. And, they were a lot of them planted right smack in the center of the aisle in a huge bin. Each primary colored, hard cover book was written about a country; such as its capital, the geography of the country, its exports and imports, its people, etc.

My heart pounded with excitement when I dove into the bin. It felt like I was digging for my favorite flavor of giant Skittles in a playpen. The book on Russia may have been in yellow, China in red, Czechoslovakia in purple, etc. I recall getting at least ten books in vibrant colors, each one a different country. They became part of my "traveling schooling," so to speak, the world in my world.

Countries such as Greece, Italy, and Spain became some of my favorites. I pictured myself lounging on their beaches. Especially, Italy since it was truly my all-time favorite, every inch of its part of creation from the Roman ruins in the background to the quaint villages nestled high up in the Alps. I always made sure I packed my box of books on the truck anywhere we headed. I really didn't care if I didn't pack anything else.

Last, but not forgotten, I collected the backs of cardboard cereal boxes that featured a different Native American Chief and the story of his tribe. We'd buy two or three boxes of cereal at a time, so I'd collect as many new ones that were featured weekly: Chief Sitting Bull, Geronimo, Cochise, Red Cloud, and others.

I absolutely loved reading about where they their tribes lived, spent the winters, and overcame to the hardships. In essence, American soldiers tried to corral them into reservations. Nevertheless, they revered their homelands and sought to return. I envied them, they knew where they belonged. I was intrigued by their nomadic life since mine was similar, in that my family roamed the countryside as far north as Colorado, just as my Spanish ancestors had done. Consequently, I felt a strong connection to the American Natives tribes' survival migrations.

Face of a Country

Money was always an issue, or rather the lack of it. As for me, I was at the bottom of the totem pole to get any of it. I had been lucky not to get caught rummaging through my half-brothers' pant pockets, pillaging a few pennies at a time. That was my income for the most part. Other times, I'd put out my hand just in case my father's heart was in the "giving" mode. It didn't happen often enough, but I'd take my chances that any given moment he'd reward me something for my contribution to his labor force. He'd plop a few coins onto my hand. I would have to wait quite some time before I accumulated enough loose change, mostly pennies and a couple of nickels. But, I was grateful for any penny I found.

I first discovered collecting stamps when I was about nine. I don't recall exactly how or where, but I think it was through some model car magazines that the boys kept in their room. "Ms. Snoops" here noticed advertising ads selling stamps for FREE! The word "collectors welcomed" caught my attention although I didn't know what it meant, but I certainly knew the word FREE in bold lettering.

Nothing was required of me as a buyer. The very fine print in the ads gave the mailing address to send in the money – I'd taped my quarter to a piece of cardboard and mailed it in an envelope (for return postage) with a return address. That's all I had to do. The stamps were free. They'd mail me hundreds of used stamps – from around the world, and even some from different states in the U.S.

I could not have imagined finding entertainment in a square-inch, post-marked piece of paper. It had originated somewhere across the ocean, thousands upon thousands of miles away from me, from a "world" that entirely consumed my interests. I held it in my hand, its history, and worldly adventures just to reach this destination. How intriguing could it be to anyone else but me? Each stamp was comparable to having read a book about its country; each one told a story I wondered about – its discourse. Yet, it was another source of entertainment for me while still learning something geographically.

I received packages at Patty's farm–since we spent several months there until late fall. By the time we left, I had several un-opened packages that would help me alleviate my boredom while serving time at "Camp Caca." Aside from my reading and work sheets to complete, I loved going over the hundreds of stamps. I tried to match them to a plethora of countries, kingdoms and standing islands I had never heard of – spending hours, sorting them by country. It would take my mind off the freezing tem-peratures inside the barrack. Wrapped in blankets, I'd pull them over my head, and hide under a make shift cozy, tent. Something about staying under tents – I felt safe, at "home" under them.

There, under my tent, I "travelled" to distant countries on the other side of the world. I imagined I had as many friends as there were sugar beet plants in the fields- thousands upon thousands, and their invitations for me to come visit them were all RSVPs – imagine that! I did. I wondered about "meeting" the person who had placed the stamp on a letter and sent to a friend across the seas, or the postcard written saying "Wish you were here." I was drawn to the adventure aspect–as if I was visiting a far-off country. I wrote a true friend, a pen pal somewhere in my future. It was one of the best times spent in the damp, freezing ice box of a barrack.

My escapes came in handy during snow storms, sweltering heat, and pouring rain – but mostly for the isolation from the family. Now, I had another "free" entertainment besides yanking mice tails, collecting arrowheads, and nightly stargazing at constel-lations gazillion miles away. Collecting old stamps became my "hobby," though I didn't know the word existed or what it meant.

Stamps became a way to discover other countries I had not read about in my "green stamps" book collections. I only had about ten books – ten countries, so my extra learning came from something so trivial – no bigger than a match box. Sorting through hundreds of stamps, allowed me to discover so many other countries and kingdoms I didn't even know existed. Just a symbol could be the country's trademark representing a kingdom, a temple high up in the Himalayas could be India, or a toucan could be a revered tropical bird in Brazil.

I had no idea of how miniature works of art depicted on a diminutive stamp would be such an influence then, and in my adult life. Even though it was not my notion to collect them as a money maker - that never, ever entered my mind, however, I vowed to try and visit as many of these countries as I could.

These stamps taught me culture and history, it was impossible not to. My twenty-five cents were well invested in bringing the outside world to me.

Winter Texans... Back in Edinburg

When January came around, it was time to leave "Camp Caca" and head south to the Rio Grande Valley. Edinburg was our next stop for three months through mid-April. We rented a frame house at 1824 E. Harriman St. (now E. University Drive), and for the first three winters, I'd spend my days at home. At least, I wasn't out in the fields. The boys and Dad found menial jobs earning some money for those months until it was time to return to Ovid in April.

At eight years of age, I was enrolled in Edinburg public schools, and in 1961 I started the first grade at Stephen F. Austin Elementary. I dreaded the walk to school, a distance of about fifteen blocks each way. I cursed up a storm with every stride I took, as I walked along with other neighbor kids I didn't know. I just knew that we were headed in the same direction.

I miss my checkered dress- what a fashion statement!

Even with the mild winters, we braved very cold spells and endless drizzly days. I was utterly miserable and disgruntled. After having spent the prior three months imprisoned in foul- smelling barracks I now had to endure equally bitter weather. My lifestyle had not improved at all. So, returning to the Valley only added to my despair. It was just another desolate and grim place where I was dragged. I hated it and nothing would change my mind. I wouldn't even give Edinburg a chance because I knew I didn't belong here.

Eventually, I befriended a couple of kids. Their companionship helped to lessen my loneliness through my elementary years. Also, my cussing subsided a bit.

In the classroom though, things weren't like they were in Ovid. I was angry because we left Ovid. So, I began acting "dumb" in class: not participating, not doing my homework. When I did turn in work, it was all done wrongly, intentionally. I had my reasons why I did that. I was stuck here physically against my will.

A school picture taken that first year showed me wearing a checkered green dress, long braided pigtails with ribbons intertwined, and my infamous razor-cut bangs. In that picture I'm posed somewhat looking sideways. Mr. Cecil B. DeMille could not have directed a better shot. I'm smiling, a smirk of a smile as if to say "this is my best side, go ahead and believe that." I figured if I could fool my teacher, I could fool everyone, and I did.

Second and third grades were a bit more challenging in that by then I was farther ahead in my education, thanks to my schooling in Ovid and three months at "Camp Caca" prison, and my self-taught initiatives.

Back in Edinburg, I kept up my charade of "dumb and dumber." I did the minimal required of me, consequently, I did visit the principal's office quite often. It started to backfire a bit. I was held back one year in these public schools, but not in Ovid. Ask if it bothered me- NOT!

I brought home library books to read on a variety of subjects such as geography, science, and social studies. I loved reading about the rest of the world that existed beyond my surroundings, brought within the grasp of my imaginary mind. I particularly loved reading adventure stories with characters, especially kids involved in doing something exciting or creative. I'd be absorbed right into the book. I'd bring home library books, but I'd also bring the class subject books to study. I just chose not to test well on any of their tests.

Several times, the teacher sent letters via me, to my parents advising them of my disinterest, unbecoming behavior, and the lack of "intelligence" displayed in class. My parents didn't read English so I misread them the letter and explained to them *how well* I was doing in school. By the time subsequent notices would have been sent, we were well on our way heading north. So, they never found out about my misbehavior. I was anxious to return to Ovid, my town, my school, my friends.

Old "Bondo" was a welcome sight come April when we "chartered" our trip with that hunk of junk. We had decontaminated our lungs for a couple of months now, it was time for another round, fifteen hundred miles or so of flabbergasting fumes, but it was well worth the destination.

A piece of concrete is all that is left of the Schneider farm; laughter and tears were in abundance on this chilly day in April 2013.

Jake & Mary Schneider's Place; Ovid 1962-1965

The following year, after living on the Cortez' place, we stayed at the Schneider farm for the next four seasons. We lived in their wooden frame bunkhouse a few yards from their house. I remember the sloping roof above the kitchen area. The stove was just below the window facing east. A brown sofa butted up against the opposite wall, as part of the furniture. The refrigerator was right next to it. The kitchen's back door opened to a second bedroom.

My parents and I slept in the main room of the house, the actual entrance. I remember falling asleep listening to the cottonwood leaves rustling in the wind. Most of the time we slept with the door open, allowing the cool breeze to filter in through the screen door.

The Schneider family was comprised of Patty, with Jerry and Ronnie her older brothers, and parents Jake and Mary. Jake was good-natured, warm hearted, the jovial one. I remember him in his jean overalls (which slimmed down his looks) and wearing

The Schneider bunkhouse – our home for four seasons.

a round-brimmed straw hat. He was generous with a smile that went ear to ear. He never failed to send one my way. Though we lived on his property, he made me feel right at home.

Early spring, Mary was planting her garden in front of their house. She grew "viney" vegetables such tomatoes, cantaloupe, cucumbers, and zucchinis. Patty and I helped her by pulling out weeds and watering the veggie sprouts. I didn't mind doing that kind of work. It was gratifying and the rows were not a mile long. We'd rake the cottonwood tree leaves, clearing the way for the vines to spread in all directions, even behind the house.

Come harvest time, we enjoyed the fruits of our labor. Patty and I gathered the cucumbers in buckets as well as the ripe tomatoes. However, between the both of us, a few of them didn't make it to the bucket. Mary would can cucumbers into pickle jars and store them in their cellar. Once the corn was harvested, I remember helping out shucking the husks, as Mary packaged the cobs in freezer bags. Into the freezer they went for a short hibernation before meeting their demise in a pot of boiling hot water. Patty and I waited a few minutes in anticipation with a stick of butter in hand, ready to gorge ourselves on this summer treat.

When it came to Mary's cooking, I remember her crispy fried chicken – "to die for!" They raised their own chickens, so a "fresh" kill was tastier than the ones from the store's butcher. Her fried chicken alone would do it for me any day, but the piece de résistance was ice-cold cantaloupe chunked and topped with several scoops of vanilla ice cream, a marriage made in heaven.

Mary was a sweet, caring mom. She hardly seemed to have an off day. Keeping up with the boys, the home, and mostly Patty, I don't' remember her frowning about anything. Her hazel eyes still sparkle in my memories of her.

I think the quietest was Ronnie. I don't recall encounters with him, though he was always polite, tall, and quite handsome, I may add. He had his mama's eyes and Jake's friendly smile.

Jerry played football, so come Friday night we'd be at the game. We even traveled to neighboring towns for the out of town games. I remember the announcer yelling: "Touchdown... Jerry!" I don't recall what position he played, but he was the fastest one outrunning the opposing players, getting down to the end zone before anyone else.

Besides his athletic capabilities, he was quite a ladies' man, a very handsome fellow. I remember a blonde, blue-eyed girl came by the farm from time to time. She had bangs and long blonde hair teased high up atop her head and held in place with lots of hair spray. I called it the cotton candy do. I want to say she was Jerry's girlfriend. Jerry was probably about five years older than Patty was, and so he was the "go to adult" for Patty and me. His only sister and her sidekick were a twofer when it came to mischief, because of that he had to tolerate us both.

With only five left in the family, four who worked full time, I was now put to work in the summer months. Summer was the longest streak of work for me, as a nearly ten year old. I could hoe my way equal to an adult, and my parents were paid for it. Money wise, I'd get something as a reward: my Reese's Peanut Butter Cups or a box of Devil's Food Cakes, come Saturday when we'd go into town. However, most of my "allowance" was put on hold to buy a few school necessities.

Nothing dampened my spirits, I couldn't have been happier: Patty, my first childhood friend lived next door. That's all that mattered to me. I remember her wearing shorts and flip flops through the summer with her short hair styled in curls and bangs rolled under covering her forehead. Specifically, her famous, all-time favorite question was "Can she, Chabela, can Emma come to my house?" I remember Patty would be waiting for us outside our bunkhouse, as we drove in from the fields. She'd be smiling and waving at us. I didn't care if I was tired, we managed to play for a couple of hours until suppertime. At dinner time, Mary would come get Patty, but she'd already eaten at my house.

On weekends, the "Little Squirt" was over at our bunkhouse at dawn until Mary came over to get her home. Any free time I had, I'd be over at her house.

You could find us in Patty's bedroom, my favorite room in their house. It was the last one down the hall and was decorated with lacy curtains, bright colored bedspreads, and throw pillows that complimented and added to the comfort and quaintness of her bedroom. It was a retreat and so charming to me. I thought maybe someday I will have a room to myself, if we ever have a home to settle in. Her stuffed animals took over the carpeted floor.

I remember the first Barbie dolls. I saw them at the five and ten store in Julesburg. They were all the rage! I preferred the ones with the blond ponytails but Patty had two or three. One of them had short bubble-hair that reminded me of puffy cotton candy. Patty lent me some of her dolls, and we'd play for hours accessorizing them till their heads came off. We'd screw them right back on.

Once school started, we'd wait for the school bus in front of her house by the road. Although we were in separate grades, we'd meet up for lunch, recess, and three hours later we'd hook up again on the bus to make our way home.

Jake and Dad

Dad and Jake became friends when we lived across the road from them the two seasons we stayed with the Cortez family. Jake had offered Dad work in his fields too, as we continued to subcontract work with Mr. Kobayashi and the Cortezes. They bonded through a common knowledge of ranching. Thus, they understood each other when it came to talking about horses.

Dad knew everything about ranching, horses, and cattle, having grown up doing that work as a youngster, then continuing the same work in Texas. Jake's passion was also horses thus their connection. Jake bred certain breeds for showing and prize winnings at stock shows and rodeos.

Dad was much older than Jake. Regardless of their age difference, their comradeship was special. Each came from an entirely different culture, spoke a different language, but most importantly, they shared and maintained a mutual respect for animal husbandry, a common bond caring for animals, plus a showmanship of horses. Their true friendship was one of kindred spirits. Their commonality was evident in both men. Jake invited Dad to go with him to the fairs, stock shows, and rodeos common in the summer

My late father Raul González – all gussied up, ready for the rodeo.

months and Dad always accepted his invitations.

I have a picture of Dad standing by the back door inside the bunkhouse. He's all gussied up in cowboy attire: standing even taller in boots, blue jeans, blue plaid

1985: our visit with Jake and Mary

western shirt with the snap on buttons, and his tall "Texan hat" ready for the trip. They'd hitch the trailer to Jake's truck, load up some horses, and off they'd go.

After the Sedgwick County Fair in Julesburg, it was on to the next one: Sterling, Denver, and Ogallala, even into Wyoming. Maybe I don't remember all of the locations, but there were several others we attended besides the one in Julesburg.

Jerry, Ronnie and Patty all rode horses, but Jerry was the equestrian competing in barrel riding and pole bending.

One summer, we went to the livestock show at the Sedgwick County Fair in Julesburg. Jerry competed in a couple of events over the weekend. On our way home Patty and I rode in the back of the truck, as it pulled the horse trailer. I leaned against a very sweaty, musty smelling horse saddle all the way home. When we arrived, I stunk worse than the horse.

These next four years, were the most stable of my young life. I would not trade one moment of any given day that we lived with the Schneider family. Although we worked for them, it didn't matter to them. Their kindness and friendship is what I cherish.

Truly, they opened their home to me, and their hearts to strangers. There are so many stories that I want to share, remembering these few in detail paints the picture of the happiest times of my childhood.

In 1985, Arnie, my husband, and I made a trip to Colorado. Our son, Andy was four years old, and our daughter Lisa was ten. We stopped briefly in Ovid, to show them my town I called "home." We visited Jake & Mary. Patty and the boys were long gone.

Jake talked about my father Raul, as if he (Dad) was right there present with us. He smiled as he reminisced about their trips together to the livestock shows, an event my father truly enjoyed accompanying Jake to help him load the horses from the trailer. I was emotionally moved when Jake praised Dad – the respectable man Dad was, and how Jake remembered him, long after we stopped coming to Ovid. I know Dad reminisced about those years too. His conversations always included the events at the Schneider farm and the times he traveled with Jake. Less than two years after we stopped migrating, Dad passed away. So, I know they are at it again – talking about horses, in heaven.

Snubbed

While Dad traveled with Jake most of the time to showcase his prized horses, Jerry competed in rodeo events in surrounding towns. Occasionally, also we attended. My half-brother, Laco would take us to the fairgrounds while Dad and Jake set up. I cannot remember the town, but we arrived about noontime. Numerous tents sprawled on the fairgrounds from which vendors could sell anything and everything: from farm equipment to food.

We stayed to watch several of the rodeo events, and the competitors, including Jerry determined to win the grand prize. In between events, I asked Dad for money to go buy something to eat. He handed me a couple of dollars and off I went in search of something delectable.

The sounds of a carnival were amplified by the screams of youngsters riding the Ferris wheel and the numerous rides of terror. However, the aroma of barbeque and smoked grilling hamburgers filled my being. I had my eye on caramel dipped apples and pink sticky cotton candy, just a couple of my targets of indulgence.

I headed towards one of the tents cooking up burgers and barbeque and sat on a metal chair facing the table, which was covered in a red and white checkered vinyl tablecloth. As I waited for service, or least get asked what I wanted to eat, the workers, a man and a woman, serving other customers nearby looked at me oddly. I just smiled at them, in hopes of them making their way towards me, but they did not. In fact, the two attendants headed towards the back of the tent, disappearing behind some wooden screens, where the actual cooking was taking place. Shortly, they reappeared with plates of food and served the customers sitting at the next table. They continued to serve the others arriving. I waited, and waited but they never came by to ask me what I wanted to eat. I flagged them down, raising my arm and waving at them with the two-dollar bills. Still, I was ignored.

I felt they didn't acknowledge me – I wasn't important? It reminded me of being ignored the same way my family did. Was it just me or did they not want to serve me? I didn't know about discrimination as a ten year old American child of Mexican descent, with black hair, and olive-toned skin. George Washington probably turned over in his grave. As for me, well, I just wanted my burger.

The "Roof"

In 1961, Dad bought a house in Edinburg. Well, he didn't pay for it in cash. He purchased it on credit, and began making monthly payments to the Edinburg State Bank.

Our house in Edinburg; 1956 Ford pickup... still trucking all those years.
Pictured, my half-sister, Gaby.

Nine months out of the year, the three bedrooms, and one bath frame home was boarded up. There was nothing fancy about the house: it was built on concrete blocks, no insulation between the walls, just the sheetrock and the exterior made of wood. The exterior was painted in a dark teal color with a white trim. At least, I had my own room for a short time to myself. The most exciting part was we had an indoor bathroom and shower!!!! Finally!

Finally, we had a place of our own when we returned to Edinburg during the months of January through mid- April. I slept in the middle room, the smallest of the three, while the four half-brothers slept in the third and largest bedroom. Mom and Dad slept in the other.

Soon after, Dad's two older sons left home, leaving Mom's younger two sleeping in that spacious bedroom. One of them married, he brought his wife to live with us, and I was kicked out of my room. I slept in the living room, just across from Mom and Dad's bedroom, for the next few seasons we lived in Edinburg.

My bed on the floor consisted of piled blankets and quilts with a sheet. Every morning, I rolled them out of the way, and left them in a corner of the living room. At night, I rolled them out again.

I was enrolled in school for a couple of months, but it became difficult to get any sleep even if I wanted to, when everyone else was still up and walking around in the house. My ears heard all the noise coming from the stomping of their feet as the wooden floors echoed every single sound.

My school clothes were taken out of my closet, thrown in a cardboard box, and placed in the living room, so every morning I'd pull something wrinkled out of it to wear. I had no privacy other than locking myself up in the bathroom.

Something was always going on there. They'd stay up late talking in the living room, invading my only space. Someone would be in the kitchen having a late dinner or roaming the hallway just outside the bathroom. The sounds of flushing toilets or the shower running was amplified though the floor. I remained awake until everyone settled in or got home late at night.

Everyone benefited from living in comfort whenever they needed a place to live, while I was the one who had to sleep on the floor. It seems ironic then, that nobody came back after my father's death to claim the house or offer any assistance when Mom and I needed the help. They lived in it, then moved on with their lives. I got stuck living there trying to salvage what Dad had built for all of us in general. No one wanted the house. Everyone reneged on it. Little did I perceive that a few years later, in my late teens, I would be the one to carry all the load of its debt.

The Harvest – October Skies

October was *the* magical time of the year. The plains became a wonderland for me: the harvesting of beets, cooler, brisk mornings to enjoy, and a much needed change up from the blistering summer days of pulling out weeds. The arrival of dense gray clouds signaled the onset of winter about to descend upon the fields, ready as if to drop the first of snow onto the peaceful scenery.

The iconic Great Western Sugar Mill in Ovid.

I had come to love that time of the year through mid-November. Convoys of tractors, trucks, machinery, and the drivers congregated by the edge of the field right at daybreak, blending with the concertos of the meadowlarks in the early morning daylight.

Through the long summer days, their melodious warbles always delighted me, whether I slumbered in the canals or worked on the rows. So, once the harvest began, they sensed what was going on, it's their instinct to know of Nature's changing seasons. Fall added to their exhilaration due to the number of offspring hatched during the spring.

On brisk mornings, I stood outside just to listen to them, greeting the harvesters as they arrived at the fields. One meadowlark would start the warbling, about the second or third calling, a second meadowlark began his, and then the third, and finally the fourth, similar to a symphony, synchronizing and echoing their mornings of glory. They'd be all around, in "surround sound," a concerto of meadowlarks and their flute-like melodies harmonizing with the peacefulness of dawn. And perhaps their songs were their celebration of a bountiful and abundant crop. I think that their concerto may have been dedicated to the farmers of Ovid.

If I was in the truck I couldn't hear them due to the rumbling of the machinery and thumping of beets leaping onto the truck, but I couldn't wait to get to the end of the row, step out of the truck, and listen to them again. I hardly ever saw them, but I'd hear their "fall anthem" of jubilation of life, and it just transcended my soul. I carried their melodies in my heart.

The billowing white steam emerged from the stacks at the Great Western Sugar Mill. Its sweet, sugary caramelized smell inundated the playgrounds of our elementary school. We took in deep breaths as if to get a high from its sweetness. I loved recess time just to watch the rising steam

The beet picker.

clouds and take in all that sugar. We pretended we could breathe in all of the sugary scent to keep it from disappearing, to keep it from meshing with the winter gray clouds that hovered closely to the playground.

The change in seasons and the pageantry of fall colors was evident everywhere. The South Platte River, once a vibrant ribbon of green, began its transition to colors of gold. Then, the cotton wood trees nourished by its water reluctantly released their crimson-red leaves, quietly falling for one last time.

Adding to this excitement, I actually celebrated a birthday, my first grade birthday with no party. It was customary to bring a treat to class, an offering of celebration by the honoree, and so I brought – you guessed it – Reese's Peanut Butter Cups for the entire class. Everyone closed their eyes and put their heads on the desk. I'd place the candy bar right under their nose, as they tried to guess the kind of candy it was by sniffing the wrapper. I even experienced my first Halloween carnival that was held at school. Never had I eaten so many sweets in any given day of my life. This was fantastic! I wanted some more, I wanted some more! That's all I could think about going to school in Ovid, to experience a whole new and different life. I was the happiest when enrolled in school. I prayed it would not end.

On weekends I could get away to enjoy the last of the scenery. Trucks and machinery rolled onto the fields to begin the harvest. Saturdays, I rode with my half-brothers as they drove the trucks alongside conveyor belts that dumped the mammoth size beets on to the truck's bed. First, the beets were defoliated by cutting off the leaves. But, for the most part, it left the white beet pale and bald, with a "Mohawk" of a cut. After that, the series of conveyor belts then removed the soil before transferring them onto the truck. I remember the thumping of the bald-headed beets as they hit the truck's bed, jolting me from my seat.

The smell of moist earth infused my sinuses as the beets were plucked from the ground. I recall seeing odd shaped beets, often nature wasn't always perfect. Some beets appeared as giant dinosaur molars with the roots protruding as prongs, others reminded me of the skinniest legs I had ever seen on a bunch of fat women screaming, as they avalanched over the conveyor belts. Following that line of thought, perfectly rounded ones, with indentations resembled cellulite dimples on the cheeks of a huge white ass. However weird they were formed, the farmers always praised a bumper crop.

The farmers weren't the only ones enjoying a bumper crop. Fury critters, particularly rabbits, came out of neighboring fields "hopping" to get in on the abundance of leaves left on the ground. They'd go to town and have a feast of their own. I'd see them darting out in front of the truck as we moved up and down the rows.

Once the truck could not take on another beet, we'd drive it down to the mill and park behind the last truck of the caravan of trucks, following the road that lead to the entrance of the mill.

Another caravan of cars, the Union Pacific Railroad train sped by the outskirts of Ovid after having passed directly through Julesburg. I remember trying to count the train's cars as they sped by with lightning speed, about a quarter mile or less from the yellow house where we lived. I'd get "cross-eyed" before counting to ten. At times, the fields could be much closer to the tracks, so when the train paraded by, tracking northward to the greater plains, the conductor sometimes spotted us and blew the locomotive's whistle, sounding a loud "Hello."

Fall was just the opposite of spring, which is focused on the rebirth of life. Fall was the redemption season for the remaining months in the year, redeeming what God had already provided. I could never forget those precious moments, timeless and price-less. I treasured every moment of every hour that I had left to enjoy the fall, for it would be my last "Shangri-La" for blissful-ness, the last "hurrah" of a great time, because thereafter I'd be heading south to the Texas Panhandle.

Soon, darker clouds of a different kind would eclipse forever more that memorable time of the year.

Innocence Lost

For nearly forty years, I carried the darkest secret of my life. I would have taken it to my grave with me, however, I finally told one person- my husband- several years after we were married. Through the years I kept quiet for fear of repercussions and reactions from already estranged family members.

The Blessed Mother Teresa revealed that incident to me in a dream. I remember it, now. It was part of my early life. Months after the revelation, I was tormented by the fact that it did happen. Would I find the strength and fortitude to write about it? I had felt her loving compassion long before I scribbled one of many stories she enlightened me to write. But, it seemed I needed her spiritual reassurance, now more than ever to tell this story. She did not abandon me.

Up until that moment, I had written more than half of my memoirs, yet, I struggled with the decision of adding this memory. After months of prayer, ultimately the answer came to light. The vision once more revealed Blessed Mother Teresa – her Divine essence comforted me and reassured me it was all right– "Emma, it's your time now. Let it be known."

It was clear in my heart that I would tell everything about the incident, but relating to you my emotions, how I felt as the incident unveiled, is truly ripping at my very essence.

This happened in 1962, during our fifth year of our migratory trip to Ovid. I would be turning ten years in October of that year. We lived on the Cortez farm, and I looked forward returning to school in August. Finally, my break came to leave the fields in the sweltering summer heat. My callused indexed fingers and thumbs from hoeing would now hold a pencil.

October came soon enough. Everything about fall was magical including the harvest, gray clouds, school events, Halloween and my birthday.

Fall would render its beauty to me every year. As always, I looked forward to riding in the trucks during the harvest. This year was no exception. I woke up that Saturday morning feeling exceptionably cheerful, typically of every Saturday when I escaped to the fields to mingle with the harvest hands.

Joy was such a beautiful trait of the heart. With fall, my heart seemed to beat faster. I tagged along with my half-brothers on our way to the field. The field was not more than a mile away from the house. I remember climbing into one of the parked trucks. I waited to see when we'd get started, but the tractor pulling the machinery was just lining up next to the truck. I sat in the passenger's side, as I always did. The machinery and tractor rode right along on my side, just inches away from me.

The youngest half-brother climbed in the truck and started it. We moved in position next to the machinery. We were ready to enter the field. Our team moved ahead of the others and the machinery and the truck inched their way into the depth of the rows. Most of the fields had long rows, realistically, about three quarters of a mile each way. The time to make one round of beet plucking would take almost an hour, maybe longer. I really didn't count the minutes, but as a kid's way of telling time, I figured that was pretty close. We were on our way, those beets kept-a-thumping. I recall reaching the other end of the field, then we swung around to harvest to the next rows. Finally, we were headed towards "home plate."

Then suddenly, my half-brother began to display the most disgusting actions imaginable. He unzipped his pants and pulled out his genitals, entirely revealing his privates. When I turned to look around, he had begun touching them. He had his right hand on them, steering the truck with his left. We inched our way back, at no speed at all. All the time he touched and yanked himself, breathing somewhat heavily.

The second I saw what was happening, I was mortified. I did

not know what his intentions were, doing what he did. A sinking feeling came over me, I felt I was suffocating. I could not roll down the window, I'd be splattered with chunks of dirt and beets. And, if I opened the door I might get trampled and forked by the machinery. I was cornered all the way back. He knew damn well he had me backed up to the very end of the seat! He had a smirk of a smile on his face as he watched me. I remember gripping the door's handle really tightly, cringing, wanting desperately to escape. I couldn't breathe, sheer fear was choking me. I gasped for air. I felt entombed in a nightmare of disgust! It was an "eternity" even though I did not know what the word meant. I do today. It seemed I was in a "forgotten time" in which I did not exist. All I wanted to do was to reach the end of the row so that I could jump out. And run! And run!!! And RUN!!!! I felt my heart race uncontrollably, the pounding echoed in my ears. I frozenly endured the remaining time as we headed towards the end of the row. My hand started to cramp from gripping the door handle so tightly. I felt that any second I would be forced to leap out the door and fall onto the belts and forks and be mulched. The fact that I went into a shock and froze saved my life. It kept me from jumping into the path of the machinery.

The incident continued all the way back. I have relived that horrible experience many times since. He never stopped yanking himself until we were nearing the edge.

The other half-brother, Laco was driving another truck, though he was a few yards behind us. As soon as we arrived at the end of the field, I jumped out of the truck while it idled. Gasping for air, and choking, I managed to walk away from the truck. I tried to gather myself as I waited for Laco to get there. An eternity passed, as he himself inched his way to the edge. Finally, he pulled in and I ran towards him. I opened the door and jumped in. He asked me what was wrong. I couldn't look at him. I also had no voice. I couldn't say a word, I remained petrified by the shock.

I sat in Laco's truck until the shaking stopped. Then, I left the field, running all the way home. I went straight to my room to lie down on the bed, clutching a pillow to my chest. My heart would not stop pounding, still in throes of terror.

Hours of revulsion and reflection passed before I fell asleep. I awoke to see "him" standing at my door. He walked to my bed where I lay. I was facing him when he lay down facing me. He placed his arms across his upper body, and stared at me. He just gawked at me, smiling. I can't ever get that image out of my head. I froze, again, but I'd hear a voice deep inside of me. I WANTED TO SCREAM AT HIM AND THROW SOMETHING AT HIM!!! Suddenly, I felt a tremendous twitch on my legs, jolting me, and I sprang out of bed, running out the room. He stayed behind.

In the days that followed, I stayed as far away from him as possible. I harbored such repugnance toward him that just the sight of him nauseated me with disgust so revolting, that a bitter seed of hatred began to manifest in my heart.

Most of all, I was truly terrified of his intentions towards me. I was overcome with immeasurable fear, dreaded telling my parents. The fear gripped me, shutting down my senses as I relived those moments over and over. Would they believe me? Would I chance getting a beating if in their eyes they thought I was lying? Who would they believe? Would they take his word against the "kid's?" If they had favored his denial, I would have been victimized again. Perhaps, next time, his actions would be worse. I couldn't imagine what that would entail. I just knew I had to fend for myself and keep my guard up. No one else looked after me.

The fiend was loose, possibly stalking me for another ambush and I was on the constant lookout. Even the lightest sounds or slight movements of people would startle me because I was easily spooked. My nerves were shot, though at the time I wouldn't have known that. I dreaded night time, and often I'd bring my blanket and pillow and sleep on the floor next to my parents' bed, even if we slept in the same room. I was just a couple of feet from their bed, however, I didn't feel safe, knowing he was in the next room. The nightmares haunted me, and I'd fight off falling asleep worrying that he'd walk in on me. It became difficult to stay awake at school since I'd be exhausted.

Within a month, we'd be heading to the Pan Handle where the boys worked night shifts, and I'd be at the barracks with Mom. Some relief came when we returned to Edinburg that winter and he left the house, though he did come by frequently, but thankfully, he'd made his home elsewhere.

Thirty-some years later, as he lived out the last few minutes of his life, I prayed for his soul's well-being. I asked God to "Forgive him, Lord for his sins committed on this earth, forgive him for the sin he committed against me so many years ago. More importantly, forgive me, for the feelings I had towards him. I have hated him all these years. I ask Your forgiveness for that. You are now judging him and I ask You whole heartedly to forgive him."

When I finished typing the last sentence: "You are now judging him. Now, I ask You wholeheartedly to forgive him," I felt an incredible sense of relief, an exaltation that I had just written the truth. I raised my head up high unashamed, having exorcised what had been my darkest shadow eclipsing my life since childhood, and the angelic voice echoed in my mind, "Emma, it's your time now. Let it be known."

The truth shines brightly.

God – Sent

Our constant move to work in other places had barred me from making friends my age because we didn't stay long enough in one location. Secondly, all the other work stops were more like concentration camps, they were filthy, uninhabitable, and its residents were antisocial. Ultimately, the constant isolation had already affected me to live a hermit life.

Once more I had to survive the yearly uprooting, the disassociation of the only place and special time of the year that made sense only to me. Leaving Ovid, Colorado behind during the most memorable time of the year, fall, was disheartening, a dismal sadness overcame me, and I felt as if a heavy black cloak had been thrown over me like a fishing net. I became tangled, constraint, and taken away against my will.

The following April after the "incident" in the fall, after living three years on the Kobayashi and the Cortez farm, we finally moved to the Schneider farm in Ovid. All along fate had been leading me closer to a friend who would be ultimately my childhood playmate, my "angel" of the fields, Patty. It felt refreshing to meet someone as jovial and friendly as she was.

When we moved into their bunkhouse right next to their house I was overjoyed because my best friend, Patty, now lived closer than before, just feet from each other. It seemed we lived under one extended roof, and coming to live on her farm made it more meaningful.

Patty became, in part my savior and in part, my stability. God sent her and put her in my transient life. She would be my miraculous gift with her genuine, warmhearted spirit aiding me in my imperfect world commonly filled with long, arduous days, and, at times hurtful moments.

Meanwhile, I latched on mindfully to that magical bubble awaiting me at the end of the day.

Her zeal and passion created a fun filled bubble of a world for us that lessened the memory of the "incident" that still haunted my mind-set. Sudden flashbacks of the incident often paralyzed me with fear, giving way to a sense of feeling lost, though I never told her about it. Too often I felt incredibly lonely due to the lack of conviviality with my family because of the significantly age gap. But, out of the clear blue, my gloominess and despair were instantly tossed aside with Patty's exuberance and spunk that always boosted my spirit, shattering the gripping spell of the moment.

For the next four years, as our friendship grew, Patty and I became inseparable. Our fun was simple in nature. We often played in the fields, walked to her cousin's farm. Patty's younger cousins added to our merriment when we splashed and waded in the irrigation canals, a summertime favorite.

Accessorizing her Barbie dolls took all day, she had tons of different outfits for each Barbie and the combinations of costumes were endless. We lost ourselves in the miniature fashion world, pretending we could one day wear the glitz and glamour of the movie stars, just as the Barbie dolls did.

Our time spent together daily would have been twenty five hours or more. If I wasn't out in the fields, whatever moments we did play we multiplied that time by having it full of fun, laughter, and mischievous behavior.

However, there was always one favorite past time I cherished. We hung out by the irrigation canal in front of her house, it had a concrete cross-over bridge which gave access to their entrance. It was on this canal that we spent many a day, soaking our feet and wading in the flowing water. We had our own "water park" free of charge and open to anyone who wanted to join us. The generous shade cast by the cottonwoods kept us cool and playing for hours. The cool water soothed my soul, a "natural" therapy, so to speak.

We splurged on Kool Pops, flavored ice; I recall the yellow one was pineapple, or was it banana? The blue one was coconut, the purple one was grape, and red one was definitely strawberry. Our tongues turned into multiple colors, often black from the mixture of the darker flavored ones. We sipped on Kool Pops and waded in the canal until our skin resembled a prune, or we finished off a whole package of twelve pops, whichever one held out the longest.

The simplicity of a summer's day, or any day, spent contently on the Schneider farm could easily turn into a grand occasion with unpredictably spirited possibilities. Patty's vivaciousness boosted energy to any occasion. She was not just the life of the party, she was life itself.

"Who could take daylight sprinkle it with fairy-tale dust, cover it in Reese's Peanut Butter Cups, and miracles galore? My dearest Patty Ann could!" Her cherubic giggles kept me in the moment of innocence, while helping me to discover mine.

I realized then that making a true friend was far better than playing with my ever faithful field mice, which came in a close second.

The saying goes "the acorn doesn't fall far from the tree," and so, I envied the exemplary life the Schneider family lived. Their generosity, kindness and acceptance I received from them while living on their property gave me a sense of belonging. I felt I was a member of their family, a stray puppy taken in out of nothingness, seeking warmth and kindness. I cared about their family probably more than I did about mine. I know it sounds cold and surreal, but it's hard to gauge, at that age, how I perceived my own family.

Living on the Schneider farm was a refuge, a haven of happiness. With time, a feeling of worthiness descended over me, creating a comfort and easiness I had longed for, a validation for my sense of existence. It was their genuineness' and Patty's true friendship which made me want to seek other friends-to-be.

The B-12 Shot

Starting school in Ovid was similar to getting a B-12 shot. Hardly any pain, but all of the gain. It gave me the energy, enthusiasm, and insights to prepare for the jubilant days to come. I began to put more emphasis on coming back to school in August, to the familiar faces, treasured friendships, and supportive teachers that had sustained me for the months that I was away. They contributed to my well-being, as well. I received such reassurance from them that I was back where I belonged.

The oppressive summer months behind us, autumn would outshine all, as we began the fall harvest. We're down to one half-brother, Laco, and Dad. I didn't go out to the fields as much, perhaps on a Saturday, and I may have ridden in the truck once just to get that old feeling back. I reveled in it. Other times, my new-found friends would join me, too, and we'd walk all the way to the fields, hang out by the irrigation canals to play, and watch the convoys of trucks and tractors.

It was the familiar, but indescribable earthy scent of moist soil and freshly picked beets that permeated my nostrils. And, in the distance I heard them, the "screaming fat-ladies-skinny-legs" thumping their way down the conveyor belts, as if in a race with the "bald-headed" beets. I believed that moment was Nature at its best.

I remember looking down the field as the machinery entered the fields. It still brought back undeniably happy moments from the previous years when I rode in the truck, alongside the beet picker. I envisioned I was out in the open fields, and felt so much freedom. I was blessed to be at the right place, at the right time of my life.

The "openness" gave me a sense of release. I could enjoy fall's homecoming and the restoration of its beauty. The vibrant amber rays would radiate through me like golden rods to cast their warmth into my soul. Thus, an abundance of wellness surged within me.

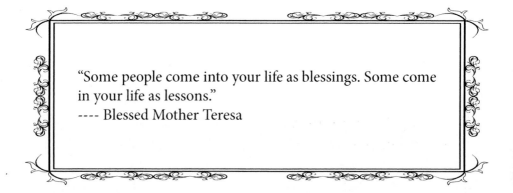

"Some people come into your life as blessings. Some come in your life as lessons."
---- Blessed Mother Teresa

The Beatles in Julesburg!

For my entertainment I relied on KOMA's nightly broadcasting that blared from our truck's speakers. Often, Patty and I would sneak out entertainment magazines from Jerry and Ronnie's room. It was our way of keeping up with all of who's who in the music and movie industry.

I'd be invited over to Patty's house on Saturday nights to watch television shows. The Ed Sullivan "Shoo" always featured the latest of rock and roll bands of those early years: Fats Domino and his "Thrill on the Hill," Chubby Checker, my "Twist" away buddy, and last but not least, Elvis and his thrusting "Pelvis." I remember the audience screaming, girls, that is, as the camera panned the audience revealing girls gone emotionally insane, shouting and bawling as Elvis swung his hips right to left, then to center.

Then, came the "British invasion" – no, I don't mean England was at war with us. It was the country's pop group bands, but leading the invasion and a new revolution in music were The Beatles.

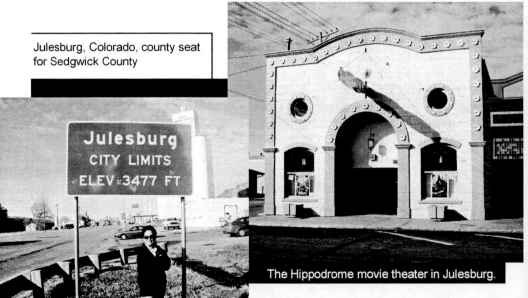

Julesburg, Colorado, county seat for Sedgwick County

The Hippodrome movie theater in Julesburg.

The Beatles' first movie, "A Hard Day's Night" was featured at the Hippodrome Movie Theater in Julesburg. I remember my excitement to go see Paul. He was my idol and Patty's, and certainly the cutest of the "fab four." They had appeared in magazines and on the television, so now it was reality to see them on the giant screen!

I begged Mom to take me to the movies. Finally, when she gave in, my friend Patty went with me. I would not have it any other way. I think Patty and I did extra chores for both mothers just to win their approval to go see the movie. I don't recall who dropped us off in front of the theater, but it was early before the show's first showing. I wanted to make sure I didn't miss any part of it. I thought there would a long line of Beatle fans waiting. Not so. Maybe they'll begin to show up soon enough, I thought. Mom, Patty, and I were the first ones to buy tickets and made our way into the theater.

The aroma of freshly made popcorn permeated the lobby. We bought the extra-large popcorn and Pepsi Cola drinks, then walked to the front of the theater and sat on the very first row! We waited patiently for the show to start, while we're woofing down our popcorn and drinks.

By the time the movie began, we were on our second round of snacks. As if two huge bags of popcorn and double super-sized sugared soft drinks weren't enough, we opted for the monster guns-- Reese's Peanut Butter Cups, doubles, each.

When the movie was over, we began to walk towards the exit. I counted about five other people leaving the theater. Patty and I staggered our way out of the theater, having overdosed on carbs, and ingested an undetermined number of grams of sugar: just short of a self-induced coma.

The Hoe Is My Ho!

In subsequent years, I still had my work out in the beet fields. Just because I started school, did not mean I was excused from work. As in the previous years, during the summer months, we'd get to the field about five in the morning, but now we had our own transportation. I'd stay at the edge of the field and work the infields for everyone. Dad's strict rule was if everyone had two legs and could walk, they could take a row and a hoe. Every person counted in the family, meant they could cover more ground, more rows, more dough (money). It certainly included me.

Dad had customized a hoe for me at the age of five. It would last forever. I never outgrew the damn thing! It just seemed to fit me better every year. Or, should I say, the hoe was "into me!" Once someone became accustom to their hoe, it was for keeps, until it was worn down to the nub. Everyone would carve out their initials on their hoe's handle to avoid arguments over whose ho, I mean hoe, belonged to.

Meanwhile, the daily grind of forced labor transformed me. I remember Ritchie Valenz' song, "Let's go Little Darling." I can hear them yelling, "Let's go, let's go!" That song brings me back memories as a kid who woke up to not a normal childhood day, but rather to days of labor. My parents and my brothers hollered: "Ándale, Vámonos!" ("Let's go!") "Dale a los surcos." ("Take to the rows.")

I robotically wandered endlessly through the rows spacing and weeding, until I could do the work with my eyes closed. Repetition builds proficiency.

Dad made sure we all sharpened our hoes every day, to assure maximum production. He didn't want us wasting daylight while we lollygagged around, pretending we were sharpening our tools. We were supposed to do that after we arrived home.

The hoe was just the tool. Over the years, that hoe was my ho. All it needed from time to time was a bit of oiling, a precise sharpening, and it was good as new. Bitch!

Life Amongst The Fields

Once all the thinning was done at the beginning of the season, the maintenance part was continuous. Weeds, weeds, and more weeds popped up. The crops could not thrive, as weeds depleted the minerals the beets needed to grow mammoth size.

We'd do several "sweeps" weeding the same fields over and over. No sooner had we finished one field, two weeks later we'd spot giant weeds flaunting their existence. Obviously, we had missed several of them as we made our way up and down each row. It was probably me who had missed a few, the times I intentionally closed my eyes, while daydreaming alongside the endless rows.

A chainsaw was needed to take down the Sequoia -size weeds, not a simple hoe. They were the toughest to get rid of because they were entirely deep-rooted into the earth and the only way to get rid of them would be to pull them from the base of the ground, pulling it out entirely, roots and all. I tried grabbing the thick stalk with both hands and yanking them with all my strength to no avail. They were monstrous. I could get to all the medium size ones, or the newly sprouted ones with my hoe.

There were times I did not want to get rid of the giant ones because they'd be hosting bird nests with baby chicks, or eggs, right by the base of the stalk. At times, I'd find baby bunnies huddled together, waiting for their mama. I felt terrible for the lost critters taking shelter there. They'd be destroyed. I cried to see them destroyed, as the huge weed, roots, and all toppled their tiny nest nudged right up to the trunk of the weed. I'd be inconsolable. I'd scream to whoever it was yanking the weed. "Se van a morir!" ("They're going to die!") It made me so angry, and at the same time, I couldn't take anymore sadness. I was crying for both, the deceased creatures of God, and the living, me. I felt destroyed along with them, but I continued living. I mourned them, weeding on.

Engine #109 – a monument to the Great Western Sugar Mill in Ovid.

The Swing Man

There was plenty of work weeding fields in neighboring towns of Julesburg, Sedgwick, Iliff, Crook, Colorado; Chappell and Ogallala, Nebraska, even in Holyoke, south of Ovid. Anywhere within 30-50 mile radius, we'd be taken to work, particularly weeding out the fields.

By the time summer came around, several trucks and their hands left because some just didn't care to take on the second phase. Fewer hands meant more work for those willing to stay on through the summer months.

If the contractor was able to contract work for his hands, say two-hundred acres or more, he'd promise the farmer he had "x" number of hands to weed the field(s) and complete the work by a certain time. More times than I can count, through the years, an entire caravan, truckloads of workers would take over the fields, like swarms of busy bees. The infestation quickly wiped the fields clean of weeds.

Similarly, too many hands on any given field meant less for everyone concerned, so my job was to claim upcoming rows for my group. I'd be the "swingman." While they made the turn at the opposite end of the field, I was already weeding the number of rows they'd take up next once they reached the turn row.

The number of acres weeded in any given season easily could have been in the hundreds, or more, but getting to the distant locations was an extreme challenge for every migrant soul that undauntedly toiled until the very last streak of daylight. It meant getting up about three in the morning, prepare breakfast and lunch tacos, leave by four or four thirty in the morning, longer drive time, both ways. It felt we had already put in long hours, without having reached the destination.

I don't recall where we had been working, but it was just outside the town when "Old Bondo" blew a tire as we headed home.

The truck swerved a couple of times before coming to a stop. When it did, it threw me around like a rag doll, as were other kids, bumping onto the sides of the thick, splintered planks. Ouch! Everyone jumped out of the truck and waited alongside the pitch-dark country road. Hand held flashlights shone faintly upon the busted tire, as men tried to change it out. I remember getting home really late that night, though it was uncommon for us ever to get in before sunset.

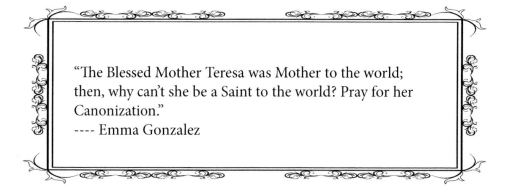

"The Blessed Mother Teresa was Mother to the world; then, why can't she be a Saint to the world? Pray for her Canonization."

---- Emma Gonzalez

Deranged Flocks

The first three years were the hardest for me. It was a rude awakening and a painful one as well when I was dropped at a field and expected to work along with everyone else, but less, and still contribute for my own existence. I was too young to understand the entire compensation process, but from the looks of it, making a living from those months just wasn't evident, not to me anyway. Monetarily, I didn't see any improvement in our nomadic lifestyle, Pop may have hung on to a couple of twin-twins (twenty dollar bills) to get us through the trips to and from.

We still hauled our personal belongings in sacks and cardboard boxes. We didn't even own a suitcase. I thought Samsonite was just a fancier name for anyone named Sam instead of a suitcase name brand I had seen in some shops.

We were at the mercy of the foreman wheeling us around like deranged flocks to do his bidding - North, South, East, and West. "Hands" that were recruited with the same foreman indoctrinated them for years with visions of the "promised land" - the carrot in front of the donkey because they were really under his absolute control awaiting his commands.

These foremen had their game really planned out, in the sense that whatever they told the workers, that is what they believed because they didn't know differently. We had to follow his orders. All these hands were "cult" members, including us, because we accepted their stories on faith as to where they would take us, how much time we would spend working a field and what our pay would be. In general, they were our "Lords" in everything and anything regarding our migrating, and, so we accepted their "Word."

Those first three years were the most difficult ones because we were under his total dominance. It just seemed to me we were in a kind of "bondage" in regards to the contract or agreement, between the family and the foreman. He called the shots. He ruled. He led us believe he was the all-powerful and all-knowing leader of the flock, and so we followed him without question.

An observation of mine as I grew up was that wherever we were taken, we had to work in order to pay him for our return back to Edinburg. I'd overhear my parents talk about saving extra money just to ensure our return. It was the same conversation every time we left for another location to go work. The word "money" was magical, because our earnings disappeared when they were handed over to him. He took his cut whether or not we had any money left over for us. I'm sure that was the case for the hundreds of migrants controlled by other foremen.

Having purchased a used truck years later freed us up a bit. We began to define our paths the remainder of the years, but not by much. Traveling in our truck to and from Colorado, and elsewhere was similar to tramping on the foreman's truck, minus the exhaust fumes and his binding contract, and for the next seven years, we trailed the caravans of truckloads of migrants from Edinburg, Texas heading north to Colorado.

We'd follow them simply for safety reasons –if any one of the vehicles broke down, the rest helped out in trying to fix it, and even transferred its passengers to other trucks if need be to get them to Ovid and surrounding areas wherever they were destined to go. Eventually, the broken down "hunk of junk" made it to its destination, and its foreman would soon begin to direct his own flock.

In all the years we traveled in our truck, to all of the different locations: to Ovid, California, to the Texas Pan Handle, and eventually back to Edinburg, I knew there had to have been costs for the truck's gasoline and food expenses. The pickup broke down and it took money to repair it. So there went any extra money that we had earned. Our profits went to fix the vehicle, to get us to the next designated work stop, or to get us back to Edinburg. Sadly, we never came out ahead.

The Pearls – Ticket to the World

My pearls came to symbolize refinement, perfection, a conventional lifestyle, unlike the one I lived during my migrant years. They were my reminders of my hope and faith in my future. Throughout the years, I'd wear a pearl strand or two to the fields.

From the moment I discovered them at the five and ten store, it was an instant connection, and their subtle glow lured me towards them. So, I bought my first strand when I was eight or nine years old.

Over time, the strands came apart when the thread rotted from daily exposure to the dirt and grime. The rings of dirt around my neck mirrored the rings around the planet Saturn. Anyway, I'd buy another strand as soon as I had enough loose change.

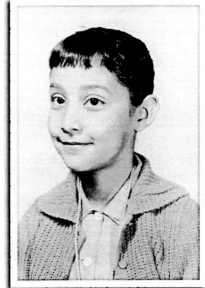

My pearls were visions of my future.

There was no piece of jewelry quite as classy as the one I fell in love with, it had a simple strand and "chicness" about it, though the rest of my attire did not compare to that of the grand ladies, the movie stars of the screen who wore them. I felt the same sophistication wearing them, even in the ditch. In time, I learned they were a symbol that represented the wealth and class that I hoped to achieve one day.

At that age, I had no idea what the etiquette was on wearing pearls, all I knew is that they had cast a spell on me - mystical and spiritual in nature. From that point on, I believed what they meant to me– my rewards would be far above the depths of these ditches I lived in.

My lifestyle was such a contrast to the significance of success and prosperity that is associated with pearls– symbols of luxury and wealth. Over the years I continued to wear my faux strands as a motivator to succeed, to strive for a better life, and to keep reminding myself as I struggled on that lonely quest.

If I kept my spirits high, I would probably make it through the day, that's how I made it through every day. No matter how much I envisioned a brighter future, each day was a challenge. I had countless doubts, who doesn't? Mine were over that ten year span. But for a youngster, it is easily compounded into centuries. I envisioned traveling on a path of my own choosing, which was not in sync with my family's way of life. Certainly, this could mean deceiving them, or was this a test of my will not to follow them at all?

Age wise, I felt much older, brought on by the experiences I was living. I thought about the worldly possibilities once I escaped from this "twilight zone" of labor and neglect. I envisioned what the Good Lord had in store for me, the potential was incalculable. How my life began was not as important as to where I would take it, or how it would end. I reassured myself to believe, to drive it through. I would choose for myself - there was no other way.

Working the fields was noble work to my family. It was their only means of support given the limited options they had, it was their logical path. Just because I had been born into their way of life, it didn't mean I would follow them. I realized I would not assume their nomadic lifestyle, as each year I distanced myself from them, more and more. Time and direction had pushed me further and further away from their lives, even after they quit migrating.

It all had to do with my desire for an education. That desire had the most profound effect on my life because not only did I choose an education, I fought for it. My long, persistent struggle was well worth the outcome. It opened up the world to me and I began to visualize the untouched potentials within my reach. More importantly, encouragement from my early teachers in Ovid sent my visions soaring, fueling my drive, leaving behind all that I would NOT become. I couldn't have known at the time how my life would turn out. I just knew it would be extraordinary.

Living in a fantasy world in my early years truly saved my sanity. The isolation tried to crush my adolescent spirit, but my heart clung to a ray of light. My pearls represented that hope. Perhaps they were my icons of determination to overcoming those obstacles, I wore them for that reason: to commemorate my future achievements.

I discovered that the Roman Empire held pearls in such a high esteem, the poor were prohibited from wearing them as being "unworthy." In the Christian contexts, pearls were used to represent God's heavenly kingdom. I roamed on His earthly kingdom without a doubt surely He approved of my faux pearl necklaces. I would achieve His successful purpose for my life– I believe I earned a strand of the real ones.

La Familia

Mom and Dad met in Garza-Valdez, Tamaulipas, Mexico. Mom lived there when her husband was shot. Dad lived nearby in La Rosita, Tamaulipas. Within their life's turmoil and mishaps, fate crossed their paths and they would build a life together.

In the 1940s, impoverished, they made their way to the U.S. in hopes of a better life, in search of the so-called "American Dream." They brought with them all the hope that could fill their hearts, but lacked skills or a trade, so they were fit for only one thing: field labor. They married in Raymondville, Texas and legally obtain citizenship for the entire family.

My parents lacked the education they were entitled to in Mexico, but they learned enough to get by. Neither parent went higher than the third or fourth grade in Mexico's schools. They were needed in the work force so their parents sent them out to work the farms, fields and ranches, especially Dad. Mom, well she eloped at fourteen, which meant no more schooling for her.

We were a blended family from the start. My father, Raul González was a widower with seven children and seventeen years older than my mother, Maria Isabel Ornelas, a widow with three kids of her own. Mom had three children by the time she was eighteen or nineteen.

Nevertheless, combined twelve people could work. Eventually, as the younger ones came of age, they would bring in quite enough to survive and then some. However, these children also lacked education. They worked in the trades that they were exposed to, the fields.

Between the 1940s and 1950s they lived in many places in South Texas within a twenty mile radius from the previous location. They had no means to travel, nor did they have a vehicle. So, when the opportunity presented itself, somehow they managed to move to wherever they found work. Dad didn't start out working the fields, but he did ranch work in Mexico. At a very young age, he'd learn the trade of ranching, taking care of farm animals.

When they settled in San Manuel, Texas he began working on a ranch owned by a tycoon-cattle rancher named Paul Wimberley and was responsible for thousands of brush acreage of cactus and mesquite infested terrain, where a thousand– plus cows happily roamed. He was the ranch foreman overseeing the cattle spread.

It wasn't until ten years later or so, in 1952 that I was born into this poverty-stricken family. I sure as heck didn't ask to be born into this group, that's

Me at one year old, with baby doe at the Paul Wimberley Ranch, San Manuel, Texas.

what I meant by "higher forces." I cannot call it destiny by choice, rather universal fate, but I do believe God, as part of His scheme on a much grander scale sealed this fate for me. He's the one to answer that question when in time, we meet.

On a Sunday, at the Paul Wimberley bunkhouse, which housed twelve people, plus lucky number thirteen --- I was born! Sunday evening my Mom went into labor and my Dad set out in search of the midwife, a Mrs. Anzaldua who lived in Hargill, Texas, a rural community near San Manuel. Dad walked several miles to the neighboring ranch, El Guajolote, owned by Merardo and Maria Celia Porras, who later baptized me.

They drove him to Hargill to get the midwife. She was in Sunday's church service. By the time he found her and brought her to the ranch, I was already born. Mom gave birth to me all by herself. The midwife found me gagging in a puddle of fluid, the placenta and the umbilical cord still attached, as my Mom tried to keep me from suffocating.

I was named "Emma" after my Dad's oldest sister who raised him as a newborn, when his mother Rosita passed away soon after giving birth to him. He was the baby of his family, and his father, Victor looked to his oldest to care for Raul. She raised him, and I remember Dad telling me that he loved her as his mother, thus he named me in her honor.

As the missing link, I united the two families. With that many kids, they wanted the image of one united family, with no difference in last names. I suppose living in such remote area, the chances of "spilling the beans" in local conversations would almost be nil. The secret could remain within the "wild bunch" living in the backwoods of a huge ranch. However, that wasn't the case. Most of the kids, with the exception of Dad's four oldest, the rest of the wild bunch being school aged, had to attend school. I can imagine the situation with the school's registrar with that many kids to keep track of who had what last name. Still, not one of them graduated from high school, however, they had some schooling before setting out to work in whatever they could find, mostly field work.

His kids were in their teens, a few years younger than Mom. Her youngest boy was about ten years old. By the time I was born, or shortly thereafter, Dad's five oldest, four half-sisters and the oldest half-brother, had married and moved away. I didn't get to know them until many years later. They moved far away. Two of them moved to Laredo, Texas and others were scattered throughout the state.

Visitations were very few and far between. I grew up knowing that I had half-siblings living somewhere on this Earth, but that meant nothing to me. However, someone once told me that family, whether you accept them or not into your life, are taken with you in the experiences you live because ancestors and kinfolk are very much a part of your life. We shared DNA and cultural heritage, but that is all. It was the González bunch - His, Hers and OURS!

Dances with Sioux

From the years of working the fields in Ovid and the surrounding areas, we became familiar with the area, the bordering states to Colorado were Wyoming, to the north, northwest, and Nebraska directly east. Ovid was right by the Nebraska border.

The first time I saw Sioux, Native Americans was in Ogallala, Nebraska, about thirty miles or so from Ovid. This was in sixty-two or sixty-three, I think. Originally, we'd been working the fields near Ogallala, and as we drove in through town, we stopped at a Sioux trading post. The store wasn't very roomy, but once inside, we noticed wall to wall merchandise in Native designs: t-shirts, colorful ponchos with bead work, moccasins, hunting bows, jewelry, and wool blankets. Every nook and corner was filled. The smell of leather permeated everything. Their creativity and talents could be seen in the paintings of mountainous terrains, wildlife, rivers and streams, or in the uniquely designed carved wooden statutes of animals, such as wolves, deer, and buffalo. I vividly remember the glass encased jewelry displays. I can't begin to describe the most beautiful pieces of jewelry I had ever seen.

Up until then, I had only shopped the five and ten cent shops. No comparison. This store had chunks of vibrant teal colored stones set in bracelets, necklaces, and rings. I had no idea what this magnificent, blue stone would be until years later: Turquoise. On the counter, sat woven baskets filled with rings, bracelets made from a glistening rock, brown stones sparkled with specs of gold. It appeared to have real gold bits within the stone.

I stepped through the opened back door to an uncovered patio, a sitting area. A few wooden benches outlined an area, sort of in a circular way. The center displayed an open sunken fire pit. I had no idea what that was for. A man approached me while I looked around outside. He wore a brown leather jacket, with leather fringes dangling from his sleeves. His somewhat tanned face was friendly and he smiled at me, his long jet-black hair pulled back in a braid. Huh! We shared something. He spoke English, as we greeted each other. Quickly, I scurried back inside the store.

At some point, we returned to Ogallala, this time on a weekend. We went back to the trading post, and for the first time, I observed a group of Sioux Indians in their native attire, long headdresses with colorful feathers worn on their heads. Some of the men had smeared black streaks across the cheeks, just below the eyes, their tanned skin was evidence of too much sun. Several of the members sat on the benches, played instruments, and sang, rather chanted in their native language, perhaps resonating spiritual songs. Four men danced rhythmically to music with a definite drumbeat, as they made their way around the lit fire pit.

Women stood by the benches in solemn presence. They bowed their heads as they chanted, in a trance or prayer meditation. It was an incredibly emotional experience of a lifetime since I had only read about Chief Sitting Bull and other American Native Chieftains from the backs of cardboard cereal boxes that I had collected. Here I was, experiencing an unforgettable event, a connection, spiritual in nature.

When the ritual was over, I learned this group came from their home in the Dakotas every summer. A group of Sioux made Ogallala their home, running the trading post. However, far from home, they brought their religious prayers and customs for worshiping with them. This dance around the fire symbolized life, ongoing, even after earthly death.

I clamored and begged my parents to buy me one of the shimmering/brown gold speckle stone rings from the hundreds displayed in the baskets showcased on the counter. It mattered so much to me that I'd walk away with a reminder of this unique mystical display. Whatever I had learned from the backs of cereal boxes about Native American tribes, could not compare to the actual observance. I felt a deep connection with them.

We returned another time to see them perform that summer. Their native rituals and spiritualism again stirred me. More importantly, it was their devotion and fervor, the reverberation of their chanting that arose from their soul to my soul. They worshiped with such passion. Even though I didn't understand anything of what was chanted in their worships and praises, it was evident they were one with God. Their ancient beliefs were intact, circling around the fire, symbolic of death and rebirth as one continuous life cycle. I could feel their rhythms reverberating on my chest, although they never looked up to see me, as they made their way around the fire. I stood directly in front of the pit. Never did they glance at the rest of the audience observing them, mesmerized by the intensity of their rituals.

Whatever they chanted about touched me deeply. This was a spiritual encounter for me, something that was true and real. Just a year earlier, I had my first communion back in Texas. I remember I memorized all the prayers, the Ten Commandments, and other tidbits of Catholicism, without coming away with a real "meaning" of any of it. Perhaps I was too young to have comprehended everything in a very short period. I think the main meaning was emphasized, in a manner of speaking, throughout all of the teachings and in clearly guided directions to live my life. I knew that I was to do right. Period. Therefore, praying to God, the same "God" of the Sioux was more than enough for me to understand.

At ten or eleven years old, certain things are self-evident, clearly the result of my nomadic life up to that point. Traveling from place to place just surviving, working to contribute, and yet, fending for myself made me wise beyond my years.

I shared the Sioux's spiritual experiences, but also their nomadic lifestyle. Reality to them was the loss of their homeland, perhaps forced to work in the trading post, and in other ways. Who is to say? I could feel, but not express the common pain I sensed from them, yet I knew we shared a familiar grief. The Sioux looked as lonely, forsaken, and out of place as I felt. I wondered how they lived back home on their reservations, isolated and forced to survive without true freedom....the same freedom that I longed for.

Escapism

The fields, the irrigation ditches…my escape.

From the time, I was five years old I spent much of my time out in the open. It felt natural. The fields were my home, they offered getaways too, escaping from the life of labor.

Regardless of where I was taken, I'd find a quiet place for some "downtime" and repose. Everything around me was desolate once my family took to the fields. Clearing my mind of the everyday grind, I would daydream and envision wonders only remotely possible. Having read adventure-filled stories, I would hope someday in real life, to actually live them. I could visit places around the world I had read about and escape to some of the most scenic places on Earth: mountains, rivers, quaint villages in Europe, the pristine beaches along isolated islands.

These imaginations I brought with me to get through wherever I was taken. When we arrived home, wherever that was, everybody went their own way. Being so much younger, I was ignored so I did what I could for myself, drifting along. For the rest of the migrating, gypsy years, it was survival, doing whatever it took to cope with the unpredicted lifestyle of this estranged family.

I cannot say my parents did not take care of me. They provided for me, of course, but they took care of themselves and the rest of the family first. I was the odd ball, the half-breed of each, and the last of the mixed "tribes." I had merged two into one, two families joined by a mystifying, but odd fate – and I felt I was the outcast. I didn't fit in either side.

Neither one took a real interest in me, nor I in them for the same reason. It was hurtful being left out, ignored, easily cast aside. They selfishly lived for their own survival forgetting the youngest one: a five, or six, or seven year old, "la mocosa" (snot nosed kid) who followed them around trying to get attention from any one of them. There is pain piercing through me at the memory of rejection. Why am I even here? They're all grownups, why do I exist amongst them? I'm a kid left behind, a fifth wheel, useless until called when needed. Just leave her in the ditch, she'll stay there.

Early on, as the last of the youngest members left "home," I was the only one that remained with my parents. Each time someone left, a part of me was taken with them. And, a void in me grew deeper. That one thin, trivial, thread of kinship still connected us to each other, however, our paths had paralleled only for that precise period of time as migrants.

Sometimes, I still feel that aching today of those lost moments in time. I long to have had normalcy in my childhood years. My soul grieves, as I write about it. I cannot say that either "halves" didn't care for me in their own way. But, these siblings didn't display affection for the short time they lived at home. I didn't feel their caring – and perhaps the absence of affection and kind words had callused this child's heart.

Today, these kinds of families are referred to as "dysfunctional." What a fancy word. I don't know if that's what we were in those years - there weren't any psychiatrists or counselors tracking us to determine that "label." During the migrating years our family was trying to survive. They just wanted to live, to see another sunrise.

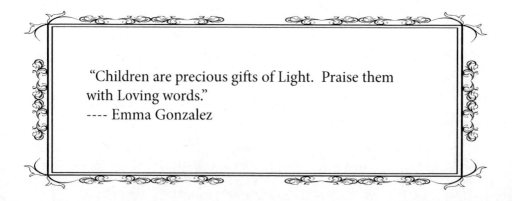

"Children are precious gifts of Light. Praise them with Loving words."
---- Emma Gonzalez

DNA

It would take many years for me to figure out who I really was. I needed to know what made me "tick" other than by God's grace. I was placed on this earth for a reason, right? I learned about my true "biological" roots – a mixed bag of DNA running through my veins: Spanish, French, Apache Indian, and a descendant of the intellectual but primitive native Indians of Mexico.

Surely, I hoped this mix would explain who I was, but over the years, I began to exhibit every one of these inherited traits. I was no longer the reject they thought I was. Rather, I knew I was a whole person, with my individual uniqueness and a composite of all of these. I felt like a daring and impulsive Spaniard-- independent, yet subtle French, the free spirit, the survivalist from my Apache roots. However, I thrived on a bolder quality – the quest for universal knowledge.

Yet, aside from all these inherited traits, I felt a sense of compassion more than any other attribute, and it would dominate my outlook on life and on people. I suppose because I craved the love and caring that was missing in my childhood that compassion became a dominating component of my adult makeup.

I recall a thorn filled past, strewn with grief, but I would ultimately be blessed with a renewed spirit. Thus, over the years, it would gradually undo the wrongs and apathies of others who had callused my heart a long, long time ago.

Nevertheless, in my early years, I still would have needed every single chromosome in me to survive. Life was unraveling mysteries at me, and stealthy challenges emerged, even from my earliest memories. I never knew what was coming down the road for this gypsy child, and so, very early on, my survival instincts were honed to an art - a "knowing," a feeling that would protect me.

"The life one is born into isn't necessarily the one that molds us for the rest of our lives. Along other paths and tracks, we encountered others who encouraged us and guided us. We are forever grateful for that moment in time when we met them."
---- Emma Gonzalez

Up in Smoke

And you thought I was done with stories from "Camp Caca?" Not quite. We returned for our fourth and final year to this infamous, God-forsaken, fecal-infested, lice-breeding, rat-infested, boll-weevil capital of dust bowls. I need not bring up any more details about the "adventures in cleaning" out the "five-star rated luxurious" barrack. By then, the giant "master rat" was in charge of handing out the keys. We just moved in.

I was rebellious, frustrated and tired at this point. I could not take the constant traveling and being sent to this hell hole to live. I felt I had suffered enough. They had no idea what they were doing to me, but nonetheless, it was the last year.

Not once did I ever attend school in any one of those four years when we crashed at "Camp Caca." My learning came from home based schooling I designed on my own. The teachers in Ovid knew when we'd be returning to the Pan Handle. Practically in tears, I'd fill my own box of school material to take with me, in it I placed reading books, math practice sheets, and whatever else they could find for me. They were a vital part of my schooling by that time, because that was the only place I went to school long enough to make friends, get acquainted with the teachers, and their ways of teaching.

I had adjusted to Ovid's culture more than anywhere else.

Three months cooped up in an ice-cold, metal dripping- water barn was my penance every year: "por mi culpa, por toda mi culpa," ("for my sins, for all my faults"). This was my sacrifice so to speak, for those months.

Anyway, the last year we were there, I was so rebellious. I just didn't know what to do. I thought of dynamite, but that wasn't going to happen, so my next other option was to set the place on fire. Now, there is a thought.

I joined other kids that were trapped just as I was at that point, perhaps they lived the same life, dragged around from place to place and forced to work. In my conversations with them, they confessed to: "no school here. . . . yes, we had school over there." They probably attended school wherever they migrated to prior to coming to "Camp Caca" just as I did in Ovid, or while back in Edinburg. This camp was another pit stop where despairing families stopped to earn a few dollars just to get them home to South Texas.

Their parents, as well as mine, didn't care to enroll their children in school during their stay here. It wasn't a priority. The fact that the nearest school district was more than twenty miles away, it is unlikely school officials would be raiding the camp looking for school-aged kids to enroll.

Meanwhile, I wanted desperately to burn down that place. I wanted to burn it or blow up every row of barracks with dynamite. Major fireworks going off so that I could see each barrack blown up sky high, with shredded tin sheets flying all over the place. Just diabolical!! That didn't happen, but it was a major thought in my mind of blowing up things. Seriously, I was about to explode myself! Psychologically.

There were some kids I knew from past years and I kept my distance from them, you know why. They turned mischievous that year and so did I, in the sense that my anger, frustrations, and disappointments and hurtfulness --- everything combined had turned me into a ticking time bomb.

The flammable cotton stalks surrounded the entire neighborhood. They bloomed beautifully, but now they were dried up, windblown by the dustbowls. There was plenty of "firewood," so we went and gathered some with a few plumes still attached. We could set off all those suckers on fire. And we did!

We lit up one empty barrack. We went into one in the center rows that was empty, filthy and full of trash with plenty of cardboard. We brought in some dried stalks and cotton balls and piled them in a mound on the cement floor, right in the middle of the barrack. We lit them. We kept adding fuel to the fire from all the trash around, it was a huge bon fire! Whatever we needed, it was there for the taking to make it count. Smoke was oozing out through perforated holes in the walls, under the door, and up through the roof. The punctured walls spewed out smoke, a fumigation gone wild, out of control. It was a major triumph in the sense of letting out frustrations. We started choking in there thinking we could handle the fire, but we ran out of there like bats flushed out by the smoke.

I don't think any one of us ever confessed, or implicated one another, but I knew very well I had done something really bad. We had that innocent look on our faces, as we stood around, looking at each other as people gathered at our "great smoke out." They all wondered how the fire started. We kind of went –hm,hm,hm and rolled over our eyes a few times and then we went home. The darn thing never burned down! How could it? There was nothing flammable inside just tin sheets on all the walls and two by fours holding up the sheets. Luckily, the fire never spread close to the wooden frame.

I could feel the frustrations building up every year we came to live in that "poo-poo" of a hole. For four years, it was the same old, same old for me. Prison time, with frustration and depression, nothing short of being detained in a "juvenile" detention camp, not only for me but for the hundreds of other kids living the same lifestyle. I befriended these hoodlums whom I didn't care for, but shared in their frustrations too. I lashed out and let out my dissatisfaction that one day. This time no party hats were handed out.

That was interesting. It was the beginning of an ominous irritable mood brewing within me. Add to it the times I was left out in the field, the unwanted feeling, abandoned.

These four years in the barracks took its toll on me. There was no way to escape them other than running away.

I cannot begin to understand how so many families would have withstood that type of lifestyle. How was it affecting kids my age? There were a lot of kids in that camp living under those circumstances and in those conditions. Who's to say how many of them survived on hope, a self-belief of a better outcome for them?

I left my aggravation on that charred floor as a commemorative that "I was here!" I did "time" in this rat holes of barracks, thanks to my family's migrating way of life.

Life gets better! You think?

Civilization, JFK

After four years, we finally lived in civilization. The year was 1962 and we lived in a dilapidated white frame house within the city limits of Lubbock, just outside the north part of town. We were down to five people.

I continued my reading and working on my work sheets for spelling and math, and looking out for myself. My Dad and both half-brothers worked the nights at the cotton gins. Most of the day, they slept, and I stayed close by Mom.

In 1963, we ended up living out of a motel in Lubbock with rancid, foul smelling rooms. A door joined the two rooms we rented weekly for the remaining two months, while Dad and Laco worked the gins.

My parents were able to afford for the first time a used black and white television they bought at a second hand store. A set of pliers remained on top of the TV to change the channels since the knob handle was worn out. This was the only way to change channels. TV remotes would be invented many years later along with cable TV and satellite dishes. The signal reception was half decent, but would improve if the "bunny" ears antennas were angled to the side. We discovered if we wrapped foil paper on the "ears" we'd get perfect reception. Sometimes the foil was gone because Mom had used it to wrap the nightly dinner tacos.

I remember watching all kinds of shows: Captain Kangaroo, soap operas, tons of commercials, from dish detergents to coffee brands, to toothpastes. It was all new to me. I had watched TV at Patty's house for a couple of hours on Saturdays, but had no idea of everything else airing. I was blown away by everything I watched! Wow!

Then, there was President Kennedy's assassination: the daily programs were bumped off as the news of the event aired day and night for weeks. Every known channel was airing essentially the same events. The funeral procession is what I still recall. His body was transported in a carriage drawn by horses. His wife and children stood at full attention as his body went by, and of course, who could forget his young son, John Jr. saluting his father.

As I learned of his death, I had no feelings about this man as our President. I may have missed civics class in Ovid and anywhere else. I tried to comprehend the events as they happened: who had shot him and why. It was all new to me.

We weren't up to speed on electronic media. I'd been kept in the dark all these years, and whatever TV I had watched, typically at Patty's house, was nothing compared to what I discovered on my TV set.

There was a whole world I didn't know existed, but it all seemed promising, regardless of the static that fragmented the picture. I would discover NFL football: the Dallas Cowboys. I do remember watching football games when the Cowboys played other teams. I was hooked. I actually cheered for them. When Sunday came, I was in total control of the pliers.

Besides the purchase of our first TV, we also got a radio. I listened to KOMA! They must have purchased both at the same time, a twofer. Buy one at regular discounted price, get the second one half off. There was always room to "haggle" over prices. I thoroughly enjoyed that kind of shopping, always looking for the "bargain." The radio was mine! Everyone else could have the TV.

Imprisonment at the "roach" motel was intolerable. It was a solitary life I lived, even after leaving "Camp Caca." What made it a bit more tolerable was listening to rock and roll music. Motown records began to release fantastic music by black artists: The Supremes, Little Anthony, The Temptations, The Four Tops, Martha Reeves, and so many other soul-music recording artists. What an incredible mix of music! The lyrics were simple to learn, but genuine at heart and with a unique beat: "I can't help myself... I love you and nobody else!" I loved singing along to this catchy rhythm by The Four Tops. My radio was never far away.

American Bandstand and Dick Clark would feature the first black artists of those times. I hung on to the pliers so I wouldn't miss their performances. Now, I could match the song to the artist on a black and white television.

The motel was in a vicinity of hundreds of second hand stores. Most of these shops were very old wooden shacks, probably held up by hand-holding termites! It was a cluster of outdoor shops, an "outdoor mall" of the past. I'd get my extra dosage of vitamin D just walking in and out of these shops during winter. We shopped for whatever we needed: home goods, outer clothing, utensils, pots, and pans; especially for newer pots since ours had seen plenty of miles and the dents on the tin pots were starting to rust.

I drew the line at wearing somebody else's under garments. Mom would buy new socks and new underwear, but everything else was fair game. Occasionally, she bought half decent looking towels and she soaked them in soap and bleach to kill anything lurking in them, same thing with sheets and pillow covers. I didn't mind that kind of shopping. From time to time, I had a say as to what I wanted at those low, low prices, quality and quantity went hand in hand.

There was always the opportunity to haggle on prices on a per item, or per quantity. It was something I learned at that time. I don't recall complaining about second hand store bought dresses and skirts, nor tops, either. Some were practically brand new. They sure beat handmade, mixed patterns skirts and tops from flour sacks. We'd make it to the stores as often as Mom was free. She'd take me "thrift" shopping just to get out of the room, reconnecting with "civilization." There was traffic noise, as drivers in cars honked their horns at other vehicles and sped on the asphalt covered streets, and actual concrete buildings were stores, selling something or other.

There were times we went into downtown just to window shop. I was mesmerized by the gorgeous ladies' dresses and fancy coats displayed on mannequins, but the patent leather high heels really caught my eye! The windows reflected a combined picture of the mannequin's finery and me with the image of me strutting in high heels, while flaunting my pearl necklace, a strand or two. People walked in and out of the department stores carrying shopping bags, full of new clothes, and other items. Wow! They must have been very wealthy.

I would see it for myself! There was life beyond the "barracks." I felt I had escaped from a desolate island for seasonal squatters. "Camp Caca" had been my Alcatraz.

I remember a drive-in, a hole-in-the-wall restaurant about a block from the motel: it was called "Johnny's Drive Inn." "Johnny's" offered the most generous, ginormous, colossal hamburgers. I am talking about six-eight inch in diameter in size. They didn't skimp on the meat portion either. The patty filled the entire size of the bun and then some. Their slogan should have been, "Where's NOT the beef!" The buns were slightly toasted making them even tastier. All the ingredients were evenly distributed, such as tomato slices, onion slices, plenty of pickles and large lettuce leaves. The burgers were wrapped in thin waxed paper and served on a thick plastic tray. Adding cheese was optional, however, it oozed out of the buns when one bit into it. Thin potato chips came in tall cardboard canisters, and at least two to three handfuls were piled up alongside the burger then, the tray disappeared.

Two people could easily eat one of them. Tall frosty mugs of root beer aided in the washing down of this savory find. I am absolutely drooling at this very moment, just remembering. The aroma of burgers went on until the late night hours. I fell asleep dreaming of eating one every night.

By 1964, we had become familiar with the northern part of Lubbock, making it easy for the men to get to the cotton gins. We found a house to rent. It was a brick home that was quite spacious. There, I had my own room! An elementary school was just a couple of blocks away. What luck! I wanted to attend school, and eventually my parents gave in and allowed me to go.

After *five* years, this would be the first time that I would actually attend school in the Pan Handle. I gladly walked every day to that school. I didn't mind the cold, wintery weather, and for two months I sat in the classroom in hopes of something "soaking" into my head. I don't recall if I learned anything, nothing that sparks my memory. I probably read some, spelled a few words, and added some numbers. Regardless, it freed me from "house arrest" for a few hours a day.

And something else so very special. I would celebrate Christmas for the first time ever while attending school! Imagine that. The hallways and classrooms, the cafeteria and library were decked out in holiday decorations and bright colorful lights! What a magical time of the year! It was a "wonderland" inside this school. Something I had never experienced before. I even exchanged gifts with someone. It was one of those Kris Kringle type of gifts, where you don't know who would get it. We just needed to know if the gift was for a boy or for a girl.

Singing Christmas carols was very sentimental for me because I didn't know any of the words. As the kids sang their hearts out, the words sounded beautiful, from a story of long time ago, meanwhile I mumbled away, whole-heartedly. There was truth in the meaning of "Christmas." The carols made reference to a baby born in poverty, in a stable, but He became our "King." I sort of made a connection to that story, that it didn't matter where one came from, what mattered is where we would end. It was a reassuring feeling, inspirational anyway. I didn't make new friends there as the time was so short, but my stay was a very "jolly" one.

In 1965, I attended "a" junior high school in Lubbock. We settled in a neighborhood whose neighbors befriended me from the day we arrived. They encouraged me to go to school with them. I wish I could remember the girls' names. They were two sisters, and their neighbor, "Reba." Luckily, I caught a ride with them to school. Their mama drove us to and from school. I want to say the Junior High school name was "Estacada." We'd be friends for the time I lived next door to them, but just as before, I didn't want to get that close to them. I probably would never see them again. For the most part, I had shut down my emotions from feeling friendly with anyone else. The pain of never seeing them again was too much to bear. Sometimes that invisible "shell" around me served a purpose, to shield me from disappointments, but more importantly it kept in what was so dear to me.

It's difficult to "gauge" the education I acquired away from Ovid's schools where I would attend at least five months: from mid-April to end of May, then August through mid-November, at the latest. I am so thankful that I didn't forget all I learned. I merely pursued certain subjects harder that were intriguing and captivated the theater of my mind. One of my favorites was geography. I loved to read about magical distant lands and their people. Therefore, it was the fascination and enchantment which captivated my heart just by reading about foreign places.

By 1966, I'd ride Lubbock's city transit buses from the house. It cost me a quarter every morning, and one in the afternoon. At this time, I don't recall the name of the junior high school. However I do recall making friends with someone named Connie and her brother Mark. We became friends during that short period of time, and we became lunch buddies.

Cafeteria lunch was everything and anything you could imagine served at a restaurant. However it wasn't cheap. You could easily have fried chicken, or a hamburger, even a baked potato or a meat loaf luncheon plate, say for a dollar. It was expensive. I bought a bologna sandwich and a half pint of milk, maybe an apple, or a portion of canned sliced peaches for about sixty cents.

Nothing really stands out about that year in that school. Again, at least I could get away from the house, even though I had study material from Ovid to review. I'd spend extra time in the spacious library, covered from wall to wall with books.

Reading was my true escape from the life I lived, my everyday getaway because I let my mind see, hear, and feel the moment of the story.

I do recall the school being overwhelming with spacious rooms and wide hallways. We had no cramming in the dance hall-sized corridors, even with all the lockers mounted to the walls. This was the roomiest school I had ever attended.

Regardless of the outcome in these schools, I really enjoyed the holidays and the Christmas events put on by the school: Christmas shows, gift exchanging, and caroling. Cold weather was even enjoyable. It was a renewing of my spirit, as we returned to Edinburg. There awaited me three months of trouble, I knew I would "do time" at another forsaken place.

"Los Babosos" Attack of The Slimy Grubs

I believe it would be 1966, when we expanded our horizons, enticed to work in California. Driven by the "fairytales" of better pay, my dad made the decision to skip out from the "beet" routine early summer and head towards Dinuba, California. By that time, we are five in the "crew:" the last half-brother, Laco and his wife make the trip too. By now, I am a full-fledged worker, having been initiated at five years old, I now can carry the full load of an adult.

Still, the excitement of a change in our yearly routine is okay with me, as long as I'm back in time for school in Ovid. California, here we come! I thought about all the movie stars living there, however far away they were, but, Hey! I could say I drove by their mansions.

We met up with very old friends of my father's who had lived in Edinburg. About the time we were recruited to Colorado, they were recruited to California in the same manner by "contratistas" foremen looking for hands to work the peach orchards and vineyards. They remained in Dinuba from that point on and never returned to Edinburg. We did.

Though the years, they kept in touch with my family. We learned they were doing very well, while we struggled year after year. Still, Dad held out long enough, until he finally gave in to their "talk" about the money making opportunities, working the orchards and vineyards. However, their idea of money making was not quite what we encountered.

Dad's friends were now foremen and managers, commanding a large army of people to work the fields. We'd be field hands, nothing more. They, on the other hand, had a pretty productive set up, expanding to owning equipment to harvest the vineyards, such as mini tractors, trailers, and one ton trucks to haul as many hands as possible. They had purchased attractive homes and the latest models of personal vehicles.

When we arrived, we were taken to a labor camp where most of their hands lived during the entire seasonal fruit harvest, followed by the harvesting of wine grapes. This type of labor "camp" housing was common in that valley, as well as in other parts of California where migrant families lived temporarily.

Neighbors rushed to meet the newcomers. They even offered us mattresses they didn't use. Of course, we get the raunchy ones stanched in urine and God knows what else lurked within the fiber layers. At least we had our own sheets and quilts to throw over them.

The "camp barracks" were wooden frame structures, measuring about twenty by twenty feet in size. No wall divisions for individual rooms. The heavy thick doors had enormous door hinges. A two by four plank served as the latch and it was the only way to lock the barrack from the inside. Once the latch slammed on to the groove, it was closed permanently, until a super strong being was able to lift it and open the door. Mostly, the door was left open during the day if someone was in the barrack, otherwise, once the sun set, the door was closed for the night.

Rectangular windows sat at the highest point of the ceiling, which could have been ten feet in height. The windows were kept open with a stick holding up the wooden closure– no glass. The wooden floors were made of thick planks nailed to railroad ties. However, the planks did not butt up evenly to each other and some of the gaps were wide enough to see the ground below. The kitchen area consisted of a two-burner butane stove, a refrigerator, and a long wooden table. There were no kitchen sinks because there was no indoor plumbing or running water. We kept open food containers in large water coolers to keep the bugs from getting into our food supplies.

Several barracks obtained their water from one faucet, similar to the set up back at "Camp Caca." We'd wash dishes in plastic bowls and the dirty dish water was thrown along the side of the barrack creating a pool of slush and dirty water that lingered on and never dried out. As the day warmed up, the breeze brought in an unbearable stench from the stagnant dirty water.

We had common areas with bathrooms and shower stalls, one for the women and one for the men. We were advised to go in groups when showering, for safety reasons. The flimsy shower curtains were see through, so the earlier one showered, the less chance of being a "silhouette," and we'd never step onto the wet floor barefoot. For sanitary reasons we had our flip flops on at all times.

We were warned of night crawlers creeping through the warped floor planks: "Los Babosos" were slimy creatures that resembled snails – only longer in size, albino centipedes. I don't know, nor care to learn why these creatures crawled out of their underground, cool tunnels and surfaced out for a nightly cruise.

Supposedly, they were poisonous and a sting from them could cause serious poisoning, similar to a jelly fish sting. Boxes of salt were laid on the floor. A line of salt outlined the entire area of one's mattress. Salt, in theory, would literally "melt" them to a slimy, slushy end. If they crossed that line of salt, the line of defense protecting us, they'd die in the process. Imagine the horror of trying to sleep at night, knowing those creatures were lurking right under me! And I thought we had left "Camp Caca" behind in the Pan Handle. Not quite, we were now guests at "Camp Slimy" to night crawlers. We were their midnight dinner.

As if I did not have enough to worry about before going to sleep every night – now I feared the distinct possibility that these creatures would pay me a visit on any given night. I kept my salt box close to my pillow, as sleep took over my senses. I drifted into sleep putting my trust in the extra thick border of salt surrounding me and my mattress.

Several times I remember having seen the aftermath in the

mornings of "slimers" having met their demise with salt. Cleaning the area was just plain nasty. We tried sweeping out the remains of gunk on the floor, but the broom wasn't enough to rid the mess of salt and slime. We'd have to bring in buckets of water and tried scraping the gunk with a shovel or with a metal brush – we just ran the water off in between the planks.

I thought that I would enjoy the change in scenery – from hoeing beets to a "sweeter" gathering of a not-so-forbidden fruit: peaches. Even the word "peaches" implied sweetness, innocence, and harmlessness. Not so. I was initiated, rather, taken to the orchard for peach-picking, fuzz-itching, labor. Even though I was barely fourteen, I counted now as an adult and my wages paid would equal my elders'.

That morning would forever live in my memories when we came to the land of "babosos." I broke out in painful blisters all over my body from the itch caused by the peach fuzz. I had such an allergic reaction not only caused by the itchy-scratching sensation, but probably due to the unknown chemicals sprayed on the trees for controlling insects. I was bed ridden with fever and painful oozing blisters for a couple of weeks. Upon recovering I was not forced to return to "peaches."

Ah! I still needed to earn my keep. Soon after, we began working in the wine industry harvesting grapes. That was even nastier in nature. It was back-breaking intensive labor: one was continuously squatting under the vines, plucking grapes with a narrow, curved knife. I held the cluster of grapes, cut the stem, and drop the cluster onto the ground. Then, we transferred the grapes onto a flat wooden plank. Once the plank was full, the infamous sputtering tractor tugging a trailer chugged by and a couple of hands helped dump the grapes into the trailer.

I don't think I even filled a couple of planks when I was attacked under the vineyard by a swarm of colonized bees and giant gnats. I screamed, running out from under the vines, as the swarm of bees chased me. By the time I reached the end of the row, I had been stung several times on my face and arms. I couldn't feel my face from the pain and numbness. Red marks on my cheeks resembled "tick-tacked-toe" marks with scratches from the vines in addition to the stings. I lay on the ground, until someone noticed me and brought some cold water and splattered my face, easing the pain. By the time my family came to my rescue I had stabilized some and the pain was easing up. Thankfully, the bees which stung me weren't the dangerous kind, but still a swarm can do as much damage.

I was sent home, stung, with a deformed face, while the swelling subsided. I don't recall being taken to a doctor, maybe I was, but I drew a blank at the time of the attack. The trauma still followed me home.

I never stepped into another field of any "fruit" kind, at least not in California. That state had definitely lost its luster for me. I remained at home, minding the house, helping out with home chores until school started. I was so heartbroken, realizing I wouldn't be back in time for fall to start school in Ovid.

Here we go again: new state, new school. I was turning into a zombie with no sense of direction. As for my family, each stop along the way added to their disillusionment and dismay for our future in farm labor. With less members in the family left to work, it meant less earnings for us.

I attended school for at least two weeks. I recall that clearly. However, Dad had had it with this kind of work. He wanted to just get out of that state! I shared his disgust. Everything my father was told about gaining riches was just an elaborate hoax. He was driven by the excitement of earning more than in Colorado. The "Jacksons" money bills in California would remain a dream for him. Dad never returned to the land of the "babosos." We would make it back in time for the harvest in Ovid.

Mine and Patty's Dream Homes

When we returned to Ovid that fall, we did not stay at the Schneider farm. They had another family living in our old bunk-house since we didn't stay past the thinning phase, so they hired other hands to finish the work.

I was upset about losing touch with Patty. After several great seasons, a part of my better life's experiences had ended and now I was back to a survival mode alone, as was Patty. We had shared a common bond of being the only girls with older brothers, and not having someone our age to play with.

I didn't see Patty as much, only at school. We had lunch together, and then we'd play with the dirt behind the school house, out by the fenced-in trees. Just using our hands we'd carve out and outline an entire house with all the rooms and living spaces among the exposed roots of the trees. We pretended the roots were the dividing walls, and the thicker roots were stairs leading to our balconies overlooking gorgeous landscapes of mountains and a river flowing by our back yards.

Our palaces, our dream houses were very real to us, we were neighbors. We looked forward to seeing each other during the lunch recess just to dream up new "designs" of our exclusive homes. I'd miss out playing with her on days when I'd walk home for lunch for lack of money to buy a lunch tray.

We had rented a house in town to finish out the harvest before heading to the Pan Handle. The house was about a block west from the red school house, just past the creek on Saunders Avenue. It was directly across the street from the Klugman's gas station. I recall it so well. I'd run over to their station just to buy myself some chewing gum, but not just ordinary gum. These were tiny purple squares, which came in a soft pouch bag with a pull-on string to close it.

I could see the beginning of the end of the migrant life at this point. The signs "were bigger than Dallas," but still in the developing stages. It was just a matter of time for the bottom to fall out. My premonition was correct. Our lifestyle was about to change.

The Calendar Girl

A twelve-month calendar differs from the migrant's "almanac" which noted events such as the date for-departure to Ovid, the start of thinning beets, and the time to return to Edinburg. The month of April was earmarked as the "arrival" and the beginning of another cyclical year of madness, while the rest of the months that followed were considerably less precise.

Estimating the timing of our next work move was an extremely imprecise way to determine our arrival or departure to or from anywhere. The slogan "mas o menos," ("more or less") was the answer to "we'll be at such and such place, to work beets, cotton, etc."

Whatever season was upon us, a time frame of arrival or departure was measured by the beginning of the month, or mid-month, depending where we'd be, "mas o menos."

The family lost track of subsequent months as they followed a routine of thinning, weeding, the harvest, and past the stop in the desolate Pan Handle. Those months were mashed into a long-term "forgotten" time frame, turning into a vicious and endless cycle of wandering robots on autopilot, doing one thing on command, over and over again.

There was hardly any time for socializing, spending time together as a family, eating dinner together, or going over the day's events. Any and most conversations pertained to the work at hand. Their invisible blinders guided them straightforward to another field. Consequently, the triviality of living any type of normal life was impossible for them.

All the while, I stood behind them in their shadows, silent in the midst of their lives, unnoticed. I knew my place.

My escape from their disconnected world and personas was my music. Music was a way for me to break away from their isolation allowing me to conjure up my hopeful future that I envisioned. And, so I began to mark an event/place where we lived with a favorite song, and recalling exactly what I was doing.

The songs were charted in my mind, and so reminiscent of an old fashion juke box – drop a dime in it and select the song to play, I'd tell you exactly where we were then. For a quarter, you'd choose three songs. I could tell you the season and the year of their debut, and probably an earful of stories played out with events.

Similar to time markers, each place had its own theme song. If you asked me where I lived in May, I could tell you each and every month, year after year was just a game of "ask and tell."

The month associated with the event/place would be etched in my memories: Neil Sedaka's song, "Calendar Girl" similarly reflected how my life flowed through the years.

January: I didn't start out the year right: snow, ice, and giant mice; I get attacked by lice.

February: I walked to school fifteen blocks away; I hated these schools, what can I say. No valentines came my way.

March: I'd be marched right down to the principal's office; Monday through Friday come what may; "lost" homework is my excuse; let's be clear, I failed however my first year.

April: the damn bunny hopped on by; no Easter basket nor confetti - filled eggs, oh, my! Definitely, northward bound I can be found; Old "Bondo" and I are tracking on, fumes and soot don't bother me none.

Yeah, yeah, welcome to my world, I am the calendar girl, every day of the year.

May: my teachers and friends know I have come home, to my own paradise in a dome; Ovid's folks welcome this young migrant soul, with encouraging words that help to console.

June: a summer's vacation is on my wish list, however, we're dropped at the field in pre-morning's mist; tornados and storms are on our tail, as we pray to God, "Please, no hail!"

July: firecrackers, hot dogs and red, white and blue, my damn hoe just broke, I need some glue. There's excitement in the air, with the Sedgwick County Fair; carnival rides and cotton candy, for me, it's just dandy.

August: Ahh! Relief at last, I'm off to school; I learn more than just ABC's, my mind discovers other worlds across the seas. My blistered fingers have taken a toll. KOMA rocks with Rock and Roll, Buddy Holly's "Party Doll."

September: See you in September, still three months left to remember. The skyline begins to turn gray, how I love the day; picture a cornfield against a sunset, the amber rays will light up your soul, I bet.

October: the harvest of beets, the sweet caramel scent from the mill, oh, how I wish I wouldn't have to leave, still. The steam clouds rise to the sky, with them I send my hopes to Him; I want to stay, "please, I don't want to cry."

November: darker skies prevail, my path's been marked "south:" to "Camp Caca" we return, but I'd rather go to jail. With books and study sheets to accompany me, I'll try to make the best of this place, you see.

December: Ho-Ho-Ho! Santa flies on by; no Christmas trees, no lights. He knows that I've been naughty 'cause I just tried to blow up the ugly sights. Somehow, amidst a winter's storm, Dad comes through; he brings me candy canes and pecans, too.

It's hard to believe how a kid dragged through the gypsy lifestyle found comfort in only one locality. Just as a spindle spins around in a juke box, my expectations revolved around a distant plains town. My gypsy life had discovered comfort and a refuge found in no other place.

Certain months of the year living in Ovid kept me in the light of hope, and in a finger's snap, I instantly re-connected to everything that was so familiar. This push pin on a map marked the center of my universe.

Finally, you can understand why April was the month to believe in glorious resurrections, thus returning me back to the familiar; it's this belief that sustained me. It really did.

"The Blessed Mother Teresa was Mother to the world; then, why can't she be a Saint to the world? Pray for her Canonization."
---- Emma Gonzalez

The Nonsense Menses

Childhood can be a total bliss, if you are fortunate to live without the muddle that may cloud a certain period of that infancy. In other words, had I been born to royalty, as Princess Emma, yeah, my early years would have been a perfectly lived fairytale. Nannies fill in as "real mommies" and they would have explained to me, one on one, all those wonderful changes wreaking havoc inside of me. The conversation would have gone something similar to this: Nanny to Princess Emma: "My dear, did you notice something different about you this morning? Cheerio!" Dream on, Emma.

There is a transformation that occurs in everyone's life after childhood, in my case it's called "puberty" or "the – change-physically–mentally-I-was-not–explained-to-because-my-mother-failed-to-do-so." I believe at this time, I have the right to scream at the top of my lungs: "What in the hell were you thinking, to NOT have given me a heads-up, woman?"

It happened during the weeding phase in August, a couple of months before my twelfth birthday. The morning was nothing out of the ordinary. I had a "date" with giant, Sequoia-sized weeds at some farmer's field. Imagine my excitement! I took to the field, with everyone else, however a couple of hours later, I began to feel a bit of queasiness in my stomach. I blamed it on that morning's eat-taco-and-run routine.

Taco, my _ss!

Suddenly, I felt excruciating abdominal pain. It was so severe it dropped me to my knees. Down I went, screaming and writhing in agony, as I felt my insides about to explode. Short of breath, I panted gasping for air. The pain pierced in center of my lower gut. I pressed on my stomach in hopes of farting if off. I knew I had eaten a bean taco! I lay on the ground clutching my stomach, curled up in a fetal position.

When my folks reached me, they helped me up, leaning me against them for support. All of a sudden, I felt a gush of warm fluid running down my legs. Panic set in as they moved me to the truck. When I checked myself out, blood was all over my legs, and staining my pants. I passed out.

I recall waking up at the hospital in Julesburg, lying on a narrow bed by the side entrance. After getting placed in a room, the nurses changed me out of my soiled pants and slipped on a hospital gown. I was introduced to certain "sanitary" items. Never had I ever laid eyes on them, and would not have known what to do with them, anyway. Some medication was administered, and a warm pouch was placed on my tummy. Ahhh, it felt soothing.

I remained hospitalized for a couple of days, but no one stayed with me. A nurse tried to explain to me what had transpired. She was so sweet, and she tried really hard to simplify things, explaining what would reoccur *every* month from now till eternity. I felt like passing out again, I understood this catastrophic change and the inescapable fate all too well.

When I was released, my parents came to take me home. Mom brought me clean clothes and put the dirty pants in a plastic bag. As I changed, she asked me how I was treated, but she never opened up about what I had just gone through. She assumed the nurses had explained why this was happening to me and to girls in general. That afternoon, I pulled out my soiled pants, and reviewed the mess. They were stiff by the dried blood that I decided to throw them away.

A nurse, a total stranger would fill me in on this "change" now taking root inside me. I thought I was "possessed" by Mother Nature. To me it was demonic and confusing in every regard. Thankfully, the nurse explained it to me that it was all very normal and not to be frightened by it. She explained I was beginning to grow up as a young lady. Mother never mentioned anything to me, what to expect, what to do about it-- nothing. I didn't even feel comfortable asking her after this incident. Whatever I learned from the nurse was fine.

It became my nightare for all times, particularly at school. I couldn't tell my girlfriends for fear of running them off. I was a year older than most, and they may not be at that stage yet. What if they thought I suffered from some disease?

I never knew when "it" would attack me again, so I'd carry extra undies, a pair of shorts and plenty of protection and safety pins in my school satchel. We didn't have those "winged" thingies, or the self-adhesive kind of pads back then. Ours came in giant purple boxes which contained mini-mattresses. Those pads never stayed put, even when pinned to the front and back inside of my panties. I wore shorts under my dresses or skirts to help keep the "things" in place, however there was always that chance that I would stain the chair I sat on.

More is better, I thought. So, I doubled up on the pads. I felt I was wearing a twin size mattress between my legs. Would I be forever shackled to the massive wad down there? I tried to walk normally, but I'd waddle like a duck. I didn't care, as long as I was well "protected."

And so, my freedom was shattered, my carefree days were over! The fear of the menses menace was a terror that caused me so much anxiety. Just put a bullet in, please! But, in time my fear subsided and it became a normal event every month. Well, this kind of excitement would not be limited, great "fun" comes in large packages.

The "Training Bra"

There was no doubt I was beginning to develop in all areas physically. And so the next most uncompromising situation would happen: having to wear a bra.

Surely, I felt my boobs needed covering and protection because every time I wore a blouse or dress, there was some chaffing going on and I'd pull away the top from my chest because I was feeling a lot of discomfort. Mom must have noticed that I frequently tugged at my chest, so she took me to one of the department stores in Julesburg to buy my first bra. This was all new to me because she doesn't even clue me in as to why we're going to the store. Shopping in Julesburg was a rarity because the only time she took me into town to buy something was always a school related necessity, such as shoes, or even a blouse or a sweater.

When we entered, a lady clerk greeted us. Let the sign language begin. Mom is doing this "crisscross" hand gesture across her chest while looking at the lady clerk, and then pointing at me. I thought "Is she asking the clerk to bless her, or something?" The clerk's got it right away. She turned to me and in a nasally voice stated, "Oh, you need a "training bra." It was the first time I heard those two words. She smiled down at me, thinking I knew what she was talking about. I stared up at her sappily.

I had seen Mom put on her bra a couple of times, there was nothing new about that, however, she looked as if she was donning military gear. White bandages came across her front and crossed onto the back where they snapped on. I recalled seeing wall calendars with pictures of Mexican women guerrilla fighters, revolutionists posing with guns, and I imagined Mom carrying some kind of ammunition.

The clerk brought a couple of bra styles and showed them to me to see which one I would want to try on. It must have been my puzzled look that told her I didn't know what the hell she was asking of me. She probably thought that I knew what we were here for, when in fact I didn't. Maybe it's some sort of bandages that will be strapped across my boobs. I had no idea what she wanted me to do with these things.

Thank God for sign language. I wasn't going to help her make the sale that quickly. She made a gesture trying to "model" the bra up to her chest, and then pointed at me to do the same. She pranced around a couple of times, trying really hard to help me comprehend her. I wanted to burst out laughing. If only she saw herself in the mirror, how silly she looked prancing and carrying on to make her point. I just let her continue. I was being immensely entertained.

She handed me one to try on, while she continued to demonstrate how to slip it on. There were straps on it similar to the ones' Mom wore. Aha! The light went on. By the looks of it, I am to put on this "training" gear. It resembled what Mom wore. I went into the dressing room to try on the first one she handed to me. They *were* just extra-large bandages that were uncomfortable and pressed against me. I handed it back to her as she swapped for the other one she held in her hands. I tried it on, it was comfy.

My mind was already way ahead of this game. Should I select a "larger" size gear my first time around, as these things are going to inflate before they shrink? How soon will I need to change to heavy duty straps of these military-like holsters? And what the hell is a "training" bra anyway? Training me or my boobs to do what? Stick out there and be "militant?"

It would be the beginning of adventures to protect my boobies.

Still dazed by the realization, I had just been initiated into a "bra wonderland." I didn't care for the transitional changes going on in my body. I thought it would get worse, as I tried to figure out the nuisances of adolescence in me. On the one hand, Mom didn't tell me a whole lot of stuff – now there's a shocker.

If I didn't need to know, then I wasn't told. Usually I found out for myself, because asking my friends if they were in the same situation was embarrassing, even though they may have started down that path too. We didn't discuss it openly, but we were thinking it.

It just seemed that over the summer, I was "filling" into these things, faster than superman changed in a phone booth. Now, I wore this "tactical gear" for the rest of my life!

These were dreadful, troubling, and trying times for me bombarding and overwhelming me with too many frightening events that I had to face alone.

One Fine Day

Hope! Hormonally speaking, there came a balance of self-assurance, with emphasis on other positive aspects of adolescence: an interest in boys.

Well, one summer, it happened. What is it about summer in my stories that stands out in my memories? Perhaps it was the season of heightened attacks by Mother Nature that I was enduring or maybe because I stayed out in the sun too long that charged my memory cells and overloaded them. How's that for a medical diagnosis?

I can honestly say that the cutest boys lived in Ovid. In my travels, I had spent time at the "the prison camp" in the Pan Handle, as well as back in Edinburg, Texas. I don't remember any cute boys catching my attention. Well, I shouldn't include the Pan Handle area, since I hardly stepped outside, but Ovid was a treasure trove of fine bachelors on backorder. They apparently were not interested in girls yet, but it was just a matter of time.

For us silly girls, Jane Taylor, April Lechman, Jody Lauer, Patty, and me, we had our teen idols from TV shows and movies. I still remember Johnny Crawford from the "Rifleman Show," something about the way he wore his "hat," and his voice was smooth in his recordings of songs, too. And how could I forget Rick Nelson and his dreamy blue eyes? I remember him starring in a John Wayne western movie, playing a quick-draw gun slinger. He sure had a "hot" pistol! Wasn't his character named "The Colorado Kid?"

Anyhow, when summer came to an end and we began school again, I felt quite differently in the sense that I wanted prettier clothes, a half-decent pair of shoes instead of those buster-brown-patched up shoes that I was bought. I'd seen girls wearing the shiny patent ones in white and black. I wanted those shoes! I wanted store bought dresses, too.

What was going on in me? This wasn't me, I kept saying to myself. Where is the old tomboy Emma? Those dog- gone hormones, which I didn't know existed in my body until I went into menopause (decades later) - which was puberty in reverse, but at that time, puberty was in full force. They were driving me nuts, and there was nothing I could do about them.

August was a "super shot." Cupid must have been working overtime past Valentines' Day, 'cause he nipped me in the heart, or some other part of my anatomy, but we'll leave it as that. It happened just a few days into the start of school. I now had a major crush on a boy by the name of "Bobby." I won't even consider listing his last name for fear of embarrassing him and myself.

I remember riding in the school bus when we arrived at his farm. He and his brothers and sisters were waiting by the road. Everything moved in slow motion, a matrix- thing-going-on as this brown eyed heavenly creature stepped onto the bus. Everyone else was frozen in time, and his body was all I saw going by me. He walked right by and turned to smile at me. Just one look from those brown puppy-eyes and I was a goner. I shyly smiled back. Immediately, my hands became clammy, my heart beat faster and one of my eyes twitched all the way to school. I swear it wouldn't stop twitching. The "evil eye" sees it all.

He had turned into such a luscious, peanut butter cup. Lip-smacking, yummy for my tummy.

Just months earlier, I treated him as a friend. I knew his family well, and his younger siblings occasionally joined our fun bunch. That morning, things changed. It was just a distinct feeling I felt when he entered the bus. I was jittery and had a mushy feeling in my stomach.

I didn't pursue this experience at the age of thirteen, however, when I did see him in school, I felt his gorgeous brown eyes piercing through me, and his smile is etched in my memory forever. I always remember him when I hear the song, "Bobby's Girl."

Gym Class – Shower-Shy

Let's add to the excitement of having to change out of our clothes into gym attire to exercise our growing bodies, one more idiotic thing to do. My memories take me to the fourth and fifth grades.

First of all, the gym shorts were not even shorts, they were an extension of the nineteen thirties' ladies' swimming suits that covered the neck all the way to the knees: bloomers. Ours were baggy jumpers - one piece with snaps down the front center, navy blue. The crotch hung down to the knees, practically.

Anyway, these things had me flashing back to my first years of school, when I wore baggy pants. It did seem that I had a destiny with soggy bottoms, rather, saggy bottoms. The only difference was the latter was a lot less cumbersome.

We had gym class after lunch in the junior high gym. I absolutely hated to run, jump, skip, stretch, especially after having second helpings of shredded pork and beans. Can you imagine the amount of gas build up by then? If we farted, the jumper would have blown up bigger than a balloon. I envisioned all of us girls, just as we started on our sit-ups: "Up, one fart. Down, one fart. Up, two farts. Down, two farts." The jumpers all inflated and deflated on each count.

I recall, Lord, do I remember that first day we came back into the locker room after physical education- it was time to shower. Everybody (the girls) stripped down to bare butts! I couldn't handle that idea. I had a major issue undressing in front of all the other girls.

I tried undressing in the shower stall, jumper and all, but "Dummy, me," had the overhead shower running. I tried to keep the jumper from getting soaked. I managed to slip out of them but my undies came flying off and landed on the wet floor!

"Ahhhh!" I screamed in incredible frustration. Just my luck,

I did not have an extra pair of undies with me. They were back at the elementary school in my satchel. Our elementary school was a couple blocks away from the junior high where we had phys ed.

Half-soaked, I ran out of the shower stall, slipping and sliding with my jumper on, and the panties in my hand, looking for our lady coach, Ms. Tombaugh. I found her and told her my situation. She escorted me to a hallway near the gym and threw my undies in the dryer, but the damn thing did not work.

Panic, is not the word that rattled around in my head, rather no "chones" (no undies)! I had to return to class in about ten minutes. My underwear was soaking wet, and all I had at this point was the blue jumper to wear under my regular clothes. Imagine the "bulkiness" feeling what I endured. I dumped my wet panties in the trash can. How could I walk back to school holding wet, dripping undies in my hand?

Needless to say, I was tardy. The rest of the class was carrying on that I was late. They kept asking me "Why are you late?" I replied, "Because I dropped my towel in the shower." They drilled me: "Why didn't you get another towel?" "Because that was my favorite one, okay." I muttered, glaring at them. Neither my demeanor nor my answers were convincing them. Finally they gave up "torturing" me.

Thankfully, no one ever found out about that incident, except my lady coach, yet the embarrassment was overwhelming. I wanted to dig a hole in the ground and bury myself in it till next spring.

I want to say that the teacher asked me for my reason for tardiness, I merely mentioned the fact I was the last one to take a shower, which was true. Ms. Tombaugh tried to have a talk with me about "blending" in with the rest of the girls and she kept assuring me that I was identical to all of them physically. That was not an issue, what was an issue to me was not having the privacy I wanted.

It was all new to me, however she knew I was very shy and she encouraged me with kind words that showed she understood my feelings. The next two years became so much easier, I figured out a way to find my privacy when time came to shower. When pushed against an unfamiliar situation, one's values supersede situations.

Ovid, Colorado

"80744"

is a number etched in my brain! It's the zip code of the Mighty Red Devils, the mascot of a farming community situated on the northeastern corner of the state of Colorado about a mile from the Nebraska border, called Ovid. It is rich beyond its agricultural façade.

I remember its people as good-natured, kind, and accepting, whose actions and directions directed my own outlook on life, a priceless lesson.

My H O M E!

The impact was so profound, it molded my life. Kindness and compassion was in their nature, and that philosophy stayed with me.

Not too many ten year olds, even fifteen year olds, can say that when their life is just beginning. My life had been so transitional, but at a very young age, I learned from my role models. I learned from their way of life and it changed mine forever.

Their lives were simple and deep rooted and had something I didn't have, a place, a "home."

As a five year old growing up then and over the next ten years, I became attached to the ways of this community, with greater appreciation for these farmers and their families.

Kids tend to mirror their parents on how they perceive life. But, my family had values I did not want to accept. In Ovid, non-judgmental values were modeled, giving way to my acceptance amongst them. The absence of a true friend was the reason that drew me to them. They accepted me for who I was.

I needed to connect to their lives, and be part of their ways, how they lived, everything about their culture, which was completely different from my family's. But, I knew that I didn't belong in that migrant culture. It's hard to explain the needs of that migrant child in me. I suppose I was looking for some normalcy away from the adult's world of traveling gypsies. I wanted more of the "perfect life" as seen through my eyes. I wanted what they had.

I didn't get to know each and every resident nor every farmer, however, their children befriended me, and it's through their off-spring's easy and sincere friendships that brought out in me an admiration for all of them.

I especially admired my teachers for their dedication, care, and encouragement that I received in abundance from Mrs. Spreick, Mrs. Melba Snyder, and Mrs. Joan Brownell. I remember an-other teacher, perhaps in the sixth grade, a Mr. Collins. He was a teacher in junior high, and specifically, I recall him helping me with my math lessons. His classroom was the first room on the right, just as one entered the school building through the front entrance.

Born a Texan, but raised seasonally in Ovid for ten years, I could say Ovid is in the heart of the plains, and in mine: I would claim it as my hometown years later.

I never had a sense of "home," a place I could call home. I didn't know where I belonged, until years later when I realized we wouldn't be coming back to Ovid after 1968. Then, I claimed Ovid as my home, and Colorado, my home state. From that point on, I would always say that I grew up in Colorado. Because to me, Ovid was my home.

I left my heart in Ovid and in all neighboring places and towns, certainly not because of the labor, but for the memorable expe-riences of worthiness, the kindness and generous munificence from total strangers. More importantly, for the friendships I left behind.

This wonderful community gave their support to a stranger, a lost migrant kid. I left there with something so monumental. They shaped my life.

Fifty years later I would return to visit Ovid. In reality, it would be a closure for me. I needed to reconnect, to feel that warmth from all the people I knew there. Though some had passed away, such as my teachers, and Mr. Kobayashi, I felt their presence just by stepping out into the open field - their spirits enlightened by the meadowlarks' songs I heard. I would write about that trip in my second book and about all the people I did get to see.

The water tower, with "Ovid" painted on it soared above. I looked for it as we pulled into town every April. In the late fifties and sixties my family came to work the sugar beet fields. Our family may have been one of several that made the trip, and Ovid's population easily swelled to five hundred, as these families settled in the vicinity for the thinning and weeding phases of the beets.

Downtown bustled with new faces, as they came to buy their weekly groceries and other supplies. I recall Main Street, where parked cars and trucks filled both sides of the street. The west side had the corner drugstore and Mr. Jonkovsky's Mercantile. On the east side, I believe there were a couple of cafes and Klugman's tiny gas station. To me the building resembled a doll house. I remember buying chewing gum there, mini-sized purple squares sold in cloth pouches. I can almost taste them.

Ovid city limits; the welcoming water tower.

Just north, on Main Street was the junior and Senior High School, also the Guzman family: Pete, Annie, and Nancy, I remember their invitations to their house. Pete was in my class, and I think Annie and Nancy may have dated a couple of my half-brothers. I visited them once we moved into town the last two years of our migrating life.

Fall added to the hustle and bustle of the town, too. The Great Western Sugar Mill was iconic, drawing every beet farmer within a fifty mile radius, or more. You knew when the beets were in town. Hundreds of beet-filled trucks lined the entrance of the mill, delivering a "sweet" deal, a bountiful crop. The steam rising to the sky could be seen for miles.

I will never forget the exhilarating musical sounds of the meadowlarks that welcomed us, and bid us farewell in the fall. Either way, I'd be filled with their songs to last me until the following spring, and till the end of my time.

Mr. J

The Jonkovsky store was the only store in town that I remember. We were told this was the mercantile where we'd buy our weekly groceries and work supplies. I recall looking up to a very tall man. Shoot, Mr. "J" was taller than my Dad, probably seven feet tall, by my account. When I first met him, I stood as tall as his waist. I kept looking up and up until finally I could see his face. I got a crick in my neck just following the length of his body, all the way to his head.

He always smiled as he looked down at me – we had a "thing" going on between us – with Reese's Peanut Butter Cups, my pennies, and however many he took to pay for just one candy. Needless to say, he was a kind and friendly person. Aside from owning the only grocery store in town, someone else helped him run it – a woman. Maybe it was his wife, or she was just his employee, but I recall her name being "Dorothy."

Over the years, we became friends. By the time we moved into town to live on 5th St., we were on a first name basis. Of course, I always addressed him as "Mr. Jonkovsky." He'd let me charge an ice cream or a candy, to our account without my parents finding out. I didn't do it too often, otherwise my parents could easily figure it out with all the five and ten cent charges appearing on their bill – they'd know I had been charging ice cream, candy and Pepsi soda pops. Then, there would be plenty of doo-doo to contend with at home. I had the timing down pat, usually in the middle of the month. I covertly "altered" their bill when I charged my sweet indulgences.

In 1985 when Arnie, my husband, and I took a trip to Colorado, we stopped briefly in Ovid. Specifically, we visited Jake and Mary Schneider and Mr. Tom Kobayashi. They told us that Mr. "J" and his wife had retired and moved to the Rio Grande Valley – to Mission, Texas, just a few miles from Edinburg. When we returned from our trip, I looked him up in the yellow pages, happily, he was listed: "Leonard Jonkovsky." He was living in an R.V. park for retirees who are considered "Winter Texans." When I knocked on his door, he had no clue who I was, but I certainly remembered him – even now with his silver-gray hair. I visited with him and his wife and had a wonderful time re-living those years in Ovid. I thanked him for letting me slyly charge a candy or an ice cream and not telling my folks – it had remained our "secret" all these years. We chuckled together- remembering.

A couple of years later, I tried to contact them again, but he had passed away. I am so glad that I had followed my heart and made the effort to find him. I wanted to see him at least one last time. He had been one of Ovid's most compassionate residents, who had allowed us to purchase our groceries on credit the first few years. Eventually, we didn't need the foreman's guaranty. We had liberated ourselves from him years ago, yet Mr. J still allowed us to purchase our food on credit, something out of the ordinary in running his business. He trusted us to pay him back when we were paid, and we did.

Little did I know that **several decades** later, I would meet with him. Then, ***nearly thirty years*** after my visit with them in Mission, I'd be writing about him in my memoir. It was all in God's plans. It always is.

The Last Two Years

In 1967 we no longer lived on Patty's farm. But, the bungalow was a bit crowded, now that my half-brother, Laco was married and had a baby. I offered to give up my corner of the room for them to have and I'd sleep in the kitchen, if it meant we could stay. Nope. My opinions didn't count for anything.

So we rented a house in town at 204 S. 5th Street, a two bedroom house with indoor plumbing. That was exciting! The South Platte River was just south of our house, less than two blocks away and visible from the front porch. I enrolled and walked to school every day, just a few blocks away. Misty Peyton lived on the next block, so we'd walk together to school.

There were days when I'd be given lunch money and I'd buy a hot lunch, but for the most part, I walked home to eat whatever re-heats I could muster up. You would think twenty-five cents wouldn't make anyone rich, by far, yet I begged for a quarter just to have a hot lunch from time to time. My parents figured I could easily

Above: My half-brother Laco; the Pecina's Chevy car in the background.
Below: The last house we lived in.

walk home to eat whatever I could find.

I will never, ever forgive them for denying me that minimal comfort. I don't know what else they wanted out of me, maybe to starve myself while trying to cook something within a thirty or forty minute lunch period. If I knew there would be a sandwich in the refrigerator, or left over beans and cold, hard tortillas, I'd settle for that, but it was never a guaranty of finding anything readily available. It was indicative of their neglectful behavior, no consideration that I had to have lunch at noon and they were requiring me to come home and find whatever there was in the fridge.

Sadly, they just didn't have the compassion for my well-being, let alone my education. It's a scar that I carried with me over the years – aggravation and feeling of resentment, more than anything else because of how I was ignored. Clearly, encouraging words and motivation were missing in this household. As I matured, I knew that continuing our current lifestyle would be detrimental to me, specifically to my education.

This year and the following year would be critical years. I was in junior high – sixth and seventh grades. I knew I was struggling trying to keep up with all my subjects wherever I attended school. In Lubbock I'd attend two months, in Edinburg another three months. Each location had its own curriculum, and just "dropping" into that classroom in the middle of the term triggered in me overwhelming stress. Furthermore, it put me at a disadvantage trying to fit into their curriculum - as much as I tried, sometimes it just didn't pan out. I was lost, and I would get that sinking feeling that perhaps this was the school where I would flunk out.

Year after year, location after location, I struggled to keep afloat. I had my days when I would lament about the constant changes I had to live with and the feelings of dejection. Shedding tears blunted the unsympathetic moments, and yet, I reassured myself that this would not be my life forever. As soon as I'd find out where we were heading, other than to Ovid, I cringed at the thought of attending a new school – fearful of the unknown. I faced endless hurdles especially those that appeared higher than a prison fence.

The higher the grade, the tougher it became. I tried to "fit" into the class and I tried to do well, and celebrated the victory that I had made it. I had passed!! I did not want to fail, it was not an option. I didn't want to be the "flunky" of each school that I attended, and come away with D's and F's because I wasn't there long enough to learn the material, be tested on it, and get a passing grade. But, the thought of flunking out was too much to bear. It was always eating away at me. I didn't want to leave a "mark" in these schools' records where every subject would have read-failed, failed, and failed, instead of PASS! PASS! PASS! **I knew I was better than that. I knew I was smart.**

The worst feeling was that I had no one to depend on, or look up to for support within the home. All of my half siblings had left, and my parents did not read nor speak English, therefore, education was unnecessary to them. **But to me, it was everything!**

The senior grades would be the toughest of education in order for me to graduate. I looked forward to my family, what's left of it eventually settling down in Ovid so that I could graduate from "my" school. In my thoughts and prayers, there was nothing more that I wanted.

In spite of the barriers and spirit - crushing difficulties, I managed to excel in most subjects, but math was the metamorphosis of subjects evolving faster than I could comprehend it. It didn't help that I changed schools two or three times in one year, within the same grade. We'd be working on different chapters, and on entirely new formulas, so, I didn't know if I was ahead or way behind in some of them. It made math with these constant changes, the most difficult to grasp. I worried about it, adding to my already chronic stress, knowing that I could survive, that I could keep my head above water, that I could pass each and every subject wherever I was enrolled in school. It made my learning meaningful with a twist, just short of my becoming "slightly" psychotic.

The "2 Emma's" developed a pattern with each change. The fearful, insecure Emma would ultimately lose to the confident and determined Emma. Time and again, I'd fathomed the last ounce of will power in me to survive, to "weather the storm"- at the next destination.

My studies meant the world to me, and so for seven years, I carried all of my books with me around the country. I was learning about the new world that I would see myself in and not in the current one I suffered. I pushed myself to learn and to keep up on most subjects.

I knew I had to concentrate on major subjects that were tearing away at my inner sense, such as math and science. But, more importantly, were the "ganas" (will power, desire) within me to conquer these subjects.

Reading became my passion. As long as I read, I learned and as long as I learned, I would pass. As long as I passed, I knew I was headed toward something better- entirely new and rewarding for me. That's all that mattered to me. I searched for the positive in every experience that I lived through, an evolution of self. And, I did just that.

In the end, I had to do it alone.

I would win.

Thus, my future, my dreams would overshadow my past sacrifices.

My Friends

Jody Lauer, our elementary years.

Regardless of where I attended school, I tried to make friends. It wasn't totally out of the question. It's just that time was a luxury I didn't have. If I attended school for a couple of months, leaving my newfound friends behind saddened me. I knew I would never see them again.

However, my classmates in Ovid were the closest to me. Jody Lauer had been my companion friend since second grade. Even though I had been enrolled the previous fall, I didn't quite become acquainted with everyone on such a short time of three months of schooling. Nevertheless, the second year we returned, Jody came and sat next to me in the cafeteria. She must have sensed the fear and isolation in me. As we began to converse, her soft-spoken voice uncoiled my uneasiness and I felt very comfortable being around her. I think this is how friendship is supposed to feel. We became "lunch buddies" and true friends.

Soon after, other girls joined the "lunch bunch," the bubbly Jane Taylor and April Lechman. We spent more time together on class projects, and being just friends. A couple of the boys included Ed Weise, Duane Weinbender, Kenny Sittner and my buddy, Raymond Schneider were my friends, too.

Fortunately, I remember the rest of my classmates beginning in the first grade: Janet Jones, Donna Schommer, Doris Gerold, Karen Haskell, Brenda Adams, Pete Guzman, Gary Berges, Kerry Allen, Chad Klugmen, Mike ("Mikey") Stang, and Eddie Mier.

I can still recall Raymond wearing a red plaid shirt. He befriended a shy and nervous migrant girl. I was in my first year of school. I knew absolutely no one, but soon his comradeship eased the fear in me. His smile was contagious. Our friendship would remain unchanged through the years.

Every year, I spent time at Jody's, April's and Jane Taylor's houses because

2013 reunion with my friend Raymond Schneider in Longmont, Colorado

eventually we worked the sugar beet acres around their farm. Since I worked the summer months, I never knew when we'd be nearby their places, so I would visit them for a few minutes in between the hoeing of rows. I'd get the chance to meet the rest of their siblings. It was always a fun gathering at their homes, to meet the rest of their caring families. April's older sister, Crystal, loved horses and Jody's younger sister Lori were just a part of my "extended" family. Jody, April, and Jane would become my next class friends, but Patty would forever be my first friend from the age of eight.

I didn't see Patty as much once I moved to High School. She was still at the red school house in fifth grade. Any given Saturday, I asked to be dropped off at Patty's farm, but there wasn't any time. So, my visits to see Patty and the opportunity to see her became less and less. I may have been dropped off on a Saturday for

My junior high school in Ovid.

a couple of hours to play with her, but she wasn't brought over to my house. By then my only connection to her would have been at school, but when I passed into sixth grade, I moved to the high school building that housed sixth through twelve grades.

A creek would separate me from Patty. The creek separated the red school house and playgrounds from the pathway adjacent to the football field that lead to the high school building. So I didn't see her anymore, not even at lunch time.

Dad continued to accompany Jake to the livestock shows and rodeos around the area, while Jerry, Jake's son still participated in the events. Dad's connection to handling horses probably reminded him of his younger years in Mexico when he did that kind of work. So, coming to Ovid, he knew he enjoyed this past time of his youth. It was his getaway in the midst of failed opportunities, year after year.

In 1968, our final year, we would host a new family in that white, cramped house at 204 S. 5th Street. They would take the plunge working the sugar beet fields, and in Dad's eyes, this family reminded him of his, ten years earlier when he had a handful of his sons and daughter combing the rows.

The Pecinas- Lalo, Fina, and their boys would accompany us to Ovid our last year, the first for them. I still remember their 1957 Chevrolet Impala, beige, I think. They all managed to fit in it and go cross country fifteen hundred miles from Edinburg to Ovid. In all they were six: three brothers about my age named Roy, Frank, and Lupe Rocha, plus their only baby sister three years old.

So a total of twelve people crammed into that overcrowded house of about eight-hundred square feet, with one bathroom and a kitchen. I slept in the front room, or what would be the living room, that leads to the kitchen. Mom and Dad slept there as well, while my half-brother, Laco and his wife took the first bedroom. The Pecinas slept in the second, cramped bedroom. It was down the hallway directly across from the bathroom. The Pecina boys took the bunk beds, the rest of their family slept on the floor.

It's amazing how well we all got along in that cramped space, especially when it came time to cooking meals. And pack extra food for the field. It was crazy! We had a midsized fridge packed with food that was all mixed up. We didn't mind sharing with each other whatever was in there.

I slept fully clothed because my bed could be seen from the kitchen, a common area for everybody. Still, when morning came, I would dress in my half-brother's bedroom and take off to school. We'd run out of hot water to shower. With only cold water, I had a fast and furious sponge bath.

In our final year, the river's bank swelled, overflowing and flooded close to the edge of our house. Sand bags were placed in front of entrances to the businesses just in case the water made it up Main Street. I don't recall if it rained on us, but it seems most of the rain fell somewhere up state, and the water naturally made its way into the river from other tributaries carrying the excess into the South Platte. It was exciting to see a "silvery blanket" of water extending as far as the eye could see to the south, past the river's edge. Through the years, I had walked its banks, searching for river rocks and arrow heads. Now its waters were right by me. Perhaps it had surged closer to bid me goodbye.

We would not stay for the harvest this year. I didn't know it would be the last year we'd come to Ovid. I found out the following April. I would not attend school in the fall either, and I would not see Patty nor Jody again until decades later. Furthermore, I was devastated that I was unable to say good bye to them, and to let them know how much their friendship meant to me. They would always be in my heart, but how I wish I had had the opportunity to tell them so. Jody and I would write to each other a couple of times, then we lost track of each other as the times changed for all of us.

My heart was inconsolable, the only life I knew had been completely ripped out of my existence, deeply scarring my soul and leaving emptiness in me beyond imagination.

We would head south to a town called Swink, in the southern part of Colorado to do other work, and a new school, a new town awaited me.

Five decades later, I reunite with my two best friends. *Above:* Jody Lauer Jimenez of North Platte, Nebraska *Below:* Patty Schneider Truesdell from Greeley, Colorado.

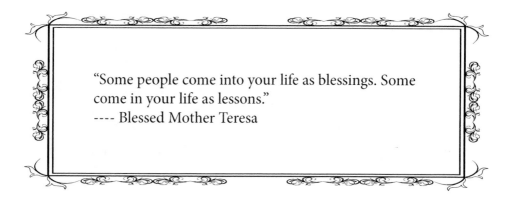

"Some people come into your life as blessings. Some come in your life as lessons."
---- Blessed Mother Teresa

The Skirt

Have you ever kept an item of sentimental value over the years that whenever you saw it, it triggered a flood of other memories, stringing them along with it? There are always reminders of the memories of great times – the event you experienced in the moment, or perhaps it was the item that made it even more memorable to begin with. Either way, they are one in the same bound and encapsulated in a time frame, where all your cherished mementos are archived closely to one another, as priceless artifacts.

I realized that if I separated the item from the moments, it would lessen the item's sentimental value: the love and the principle of having kept it in the first place. Moreover, these treasured recollections are great finds - they are my second skin. They are a part of me something I'd cherish and love. Yet, hidden deep beneath my impervious outer shell. Some moments cannot be remembered without triggering other memories that significantly elicit such joy and fondness that truly inspired the soul - the heart will treasure them even more.

And so, this is how I recall "my skirt." My navy blue, pleated skirt is the last item Mom ever bought for me during our last summer we worked in Ovid in 1968. I had been in downtown Julesburg on a Saturday window shopping, as that is how I spent most of my time when we did go to town. I did my "scouting" of upcoming fashions for the fall and I'd keep in mind certain things I'd see in the windows, so that when the time came to buy school clothes, at least I'd have one or two special items that I would beg

Pimping in my red sweater!

my parents to buy for me. Typically, it involved stylish shoes, the black patent leather loafers to wear with "bobby socks," not the Buster Brown, patched up shoes I had worn during my elementary school years. Long ago, I had "bequeathed" those Bozo shoes to trash cans, they could rest in peace amongst the piles.

In the late 60s, I gained a bit more freedom in choosing my own attire. Whatever few pieces of clothing I coordinated seemed to work out most of the time. I could combine them with older, outdated styles to revamp the look. As for school dresses, I looked for bright colors always and a cozy V-neckline sweater for the cooler autumn days ahead.

On this particular Saturday, in one of the boutique's windows, a navy blue skirt with pleats was displayed on a statuesque mannequin. The mannequin wasn't topless. She had been dressed in a red v-neck light sweater with three-quarter length sleeves. The v-neck was designed to stand out due to the wide, black, piping sewn on it. The ensemble looked strikingly beautiful on the pale, bugged-eye mannequin, but in the words of Hayley Mills,

True admirers: the plastic ducks approve of my ensemble!

it would look absolutely "gor-r-r-geous" on me! I wanted that ensemble more than the air in my lungs at that very moment. Excitedly, I envisioned sporting it on my first day of school. The shiny black patent shoes would "pull" the black piping off the sweater making the outfit complete. I stood outside the store's window, drooling at such a find-my find!

Normally, I had the chance to place the items on a lay-a-away plan, but when I told Mom about it she insisted no need to do that. We wouldn't be around to finish paying it off. We would be leaving Ovid in a few days to some other town in the southern part of Colorado to go work. I was stunned with the news that I wouldn't be attending school in Ovid that fall. I began to gasp, as if the air had been cut off from me. Now was the time for me to hook up to an oxygen mask and crank up the tank for maximum air flow. Disbelief and the pain of leaving would catch up to me when we started heading south.

Immediately, I began to plead with Mother to at least buy me the skirt and sweater before we left. I begged and cried for days, until, as a last resort to shut me up, she went to the store and bought them. Gladly, I would not bug her anymore.

And so I would bring with me to Texas the last two pieces of clothing I had begged to have, to celebrate the end of my contented era living in Ovid.

I wore my skirt until it faded to a light blue-gray color, the hem began to tear along the crease, and then the thread started to unravel. I couldn't stop it. Eventually the zipper busted, and even then I pinned a safety pin for closure: still I wore it to school. The sweater lost its red vibrancy. Faded and pilling, together they comforted me through a couple of lonely junior high school years in Edinburg - I missed my friends in Ovid.

Another decade stretched into an eternity, the time it took to make one or two best friends. I would have to start all over again.

I treasured these two pieces of clothing long after they didn't fit me anymore. As long as I had them, they kept my memories of living in Ovid alive and somehow, I was able to mentally keep going, day to day in Edinburg. I had an old armoire in my room and that's where I had my skirt and sweater safely stored. Faded and torn up, though I could never wear them again, I knew they'd be there for me any given day I needed a "boost" to my spirit. That was quite often, actually. I'd take them out just to reconnect, and then store them again. Now, my vintage garments had paired with the last fading sunsets I vividly remembered of Ovid. More-over, they would help me get through some troubling school days ahead.

Then, one day, I came home from school. I think it was my sophomore year. Mom began cleaning out the old armoire in my room. I don't know why she'd go looking in there for anything to throw out. It was my stuff, not hers. I didn't have anything that belonged to her. I guessed that her nosiness or unsettling thoughts of finding something out of the ordinary, made her rum-mage through my armoire. However, "Sherlock" didn't find any-thing out of the ordinary.

By the time I arrived home, Mom had stolen several pieces of clothing, some still usable that I wore to school, and my favorite skirt and sweater. She had given them to someone who came to visit her from Mexico, claiming to be a family member. She gave her some of my wearable school clothes and my treasured skirt and sweater.

I went ballistic! I had an outright confrontation with Mom. Our yelling could probably be heard for blocks. Without any regard to my personal property, especially clothes, and even more so my precious skirt and sweater, she had taken it upon herself to give away my things without my permission. However, nothing was resolved. My clothes were gone and my beloved treasure, too. Mom apparently didn't give a darn. She turned to me and justi-fied herself: "She is your cousin from Mexico. She needed some money, so I gave her some of your clothes to go sell. You have a lot of clothes anyway." What "cousin?" I didn't even know who she was, and frankly, my dearest Mother, I didn't give a hoot about the woman. She could have been a total stranger, for all I knew.

Most if not all my stuff was hand sewn - that's all I had, but they were mine. I had been working part time ever since we came back from Ovid. Dad's income, while living in Edinburg, dropped significantly so I had begun to pay for my own clothes. I couldn't believe the thoughtless and selfish act she had committed against her own daughter. Why couldn't she have asked me if I had some clothes to give away? Why couldn't she have given her own clothes away instead of mine? I had lost forever my tangible connection with Ovid.

Now someone in a foreign country would wear them without regard to the sentimental value that a girl in Texas needed to keep her sanity. I loved that ensemble so much that I had someone take a Polaroid picture of me wearing it. Now, all I had left was the photo of me wearing my skirt and sweater, still vibrant in color keeping my memories of a comforting plains town in Colorado alive. At least, she didn't give away the photo as well.

The photo would bring me some comfort and consolation. With it, I could relive my memories, each one strung along together, a strand of pearls – each pearl's luster glowed, casting light to the vestiges of my happier childhood years. More importantly, now they would illuminate the somber path that I would have to journey, stringing along other "pearls" of my life.

Meanwhile, my thoughts and my heart never left Ovid. In fact, to this day, they are still there, and the fond memories spanning over five decades, have sweetened with the passing time reflected in the photo – and in my long - ago lost navy blue skirt.

The Last Stop: I AM DONE!

Swink, La Junta, and Rocky Ford, Colorado are a cluster of three farming communities in southern Colorado. Dad decided he'd try his luck in this area as well. I was a fully-fledged worker by now, a contributing member. We landed in Swink, another camp of individual frame homes, similar to the barracks we inhabited in the Pan Handle since we had no indoor plumbing. Bathrooms and shower stalls were at the far west side of the camp.

Other families there carried on with their lives without butting into ours.

Just days after our arrival at the camp I witnessed an unusual and frightening incident. One of the families owned a large truck, probably a one ton truck. I remember the extra set of tires on the rear of the truck.

Anyhow, one of the siblings drove the truck – a short, hefty woman. I recall she pulled up in front of their house and then she and the rest of the workers exited out of the truck. When everybody had gone on their way to their houses, she walked over to the gas tank, removed the fuel cap, and began sniffing into the opening. She took in deep breaths of fumes emanating from the fuel tank, sighed, and then repeated the process. Several times she went on doing this. I watched in horror, wondering why she did that and what were the fumes doing to her head. I couldn't imagine anything healthy would result from it. I'd see her in the fields every day, but I especially kept my distance from her.

We would be introduced to harvesting cantaloupe, cucumbers, tomatoes, and onions. I remember getting paid twenty-five cents a bushel basket for cucumbers and tomatoes. Forty-five pounds was the equivalent of a five gallon bucket. Once we filled the bucket we had to carry it out of the field and deliver to the hands that would then dump the tomatoes on to a trailer. Each full bucket was counted when delivered, and the worker was given credit.

The foreman kept track of all the twenty-five cent buckets harvested by each individual. Some people carried two buckets at a time. With my strength, I could barely make it with one full bucket with my short strides, stopping to put the bucket down on the ground to catch my breath and strength before moving on. One bucket was more than enough for me.

It was back-breaking, intense, and laborious, constantly stooping and bending over the ground. As the work gloves harden with the constant gripping of the bucket's metal handle they caused the blisters on the crease of my hand to turn into open, painful sores. Sometimes I'd wrap a cloth on my hand before slipping on the gloves. A barrier helped some, but then the cloth stuck to the skin. Trying to pull the cloth off the raw flesh was excruciating agony.

The next crops were cantaloupe and onions. Oversized produce still paid a pittance as did the smaller veggies. Cantaloupes were placed in crates, but were hoisted on to the back of the trucks, traveling alongside the rows. I don't recall the price paid for those crates, but it wasn't very much, that's for sure.

The round, sleek skinned fruit reminded me of human skulls lying throughout the field, a massive open grave with faceless skulls. Who would have thought this fruit in particular, once chilled, could be the ultimate heat-savior, mouth–watering delight just by busting its "skull" in half and scooping out its sweet, juicy brains? Oh, don't forget to add vanilla ice cream!

I filled the burlap sacks of onions, weighing about one-hundred pounds each when filled to the top. Luckily, the labor involved leaving the burlap sack just where you had filled it, there was no need to move it. Along came a tractor trailer and hands to lift the sacks, and drop-off empty sacks to fill. I tried looking down to the very end of the row, but I saw no end in sight. I still had to take another row to return to the edge, back where I had started. I may have become delusional and perhaps saw heat waves shimmering over an oasis way out in the distance, about half way up the middle of the rows.

The dots on the horizon were human beings, as they seemed to sway amidst the heat wave. Needless to say, these rows were the longest I had ever come across, not even in the sugar beet fields. Kids half my size took on a row by themselves, others shared a row. However many onions it took to fill one bushel, everyone was in a race to get paid for their count. Thousands upon thousands of oversized brown sacks resembled giant ant mounds scattered throughout the endless fields.

Our camp was three to four miles from the quaint town of Swink. The railroad tracks flanked the town as well as our camp, and every day about 4 p.m. the train and its entourage of cars crossed the farm road leading to the camp, sounding off its whistle, enroute to the Rockies. I knew I had a couple more hours to go, at least until sundown to "pick my heart out" on whatever veggie was at hand.

I had no choice but to endure open hand sores, an aching-breaking back, and sweltering heat waves. Enough! I can't recall coming home after work during those summer days. I was so exhausted. I would have preferred to walk the weeded fields in Colorado, and keep on walking, until I fell off the edge of the earth. The familiarity at least would have reminded me I was still in neighboring Ovid.

Two more months there and we'd leave for the Pan Handle, but not before I enroll in a new school in August for a few weeks. I don't recall a whole lot about this one. But, does it matter?

The Last Sunset

I had a feeling when we first arrived in Ovid, of something entirely unique and extraordinary waiting for me. However I never imagined I'd be waking up in near freezing temperatures on a late April pre-dawn morning and realize, "Oh, shit, this is my new life and I've just been dumped in a ditch!"

My intuition of a rosy future would supersede the fear I battled in my early years, the years of migrating to Ovid, but a consciousness of well-being and acceptance convinced me that this was where I truly belonged (Not in the ditch, though). "Greener fields" sometimes refer to better times out of reach. I made the association in similar ways.

Child of the cornfield!

I had been accepted as a member of their community, I had made friends, and I learned about oceans and countries beyond the horizon, and my jet plane that I dreamed of flying was hangered just a couple of hundred miles south.

These were my riches encountered along the way. But now, it was that dog-gone feeling, deep down in my bones- a "knowing"- it just didn't feel right. Something *reeeeally* crappy was coming down the pike. It was just a matter of time, perhaps in a couple of years, or even sooner.

I foresaw a tempest threatening my family, already floundering as they clung to a thread of hope to survive, their energies sucked out of their souls, sustained by the strength of His Will. I was caught in the whirlwind of their lives, which eventually toppled us all.

The fall of 1968 was a point in time that symbolized the end for us as well.

In reality, I would witness my last sunset in Ovid. I envisioned dusk setting in, the end of carefree days, end of a happy era, and my inner sense whispered of a calamity of vast proportions stalking my path. The last sunset, viewed through the withered cornfields waving in autumn's winds, was defiantly saying, "goodbye-sayonara" to the wonderful years in Ovid, when things were "greener" for me.

Even now, every fall, the gorgeous view of the amber sunset or perhaps a sunrise against the fields steals me away to the memories of autumns spent in Ovid.

Finally, the onset of darker clouds still allowed a ray of light to filter through. Meanwhile, the brittle stalks swayed ever so slightly with the breezy winds, ahead of winter's howling, destructive weather. I knew the "storm" was approaching rapidly.

I later made a connection with a movie titled "Hoosiers," in describing Main Street in Ovid and the similarities of their historic buildings. At the end of the movie there is an incredibly picturesque view of an evening sunset, or perhaps daylight's first light, streaming through gray clouds over the horizon. The amber colored glow of the sun's rays cast their brilliance, coming through with multiple streaks of light, beaming down to a cornfield.

Whether the shot for the movie was filmed, at a sunset or sunrise, the beauty of it triggered the memory of my years migrating to Ovid. The eight seconds of that shot in the film held me captive, and I was drawn right into the scene, taking me back to a lifetime of euphoric and promising moments in time.......... I hear the rustling of the cornstalks swaying in the midst of my memoirs.

Surely, I had an abundance of sunrises and sunsets. I remember them!

Time has stood still at the farm of Carl & Eleanor Williams on County Rd. 34.

This farm is now owned by David Brandt who in 1960 was our neighbor across County Rd. 36, which is the Colorado/Nebraska state line.

Journey Unfolding

As we approached the last year of our migration, I must have been about fourteen, and I already perceived my destiny unfolding before me. That crappy feeling I had just a year or so earlier was now a reality.

My journey to labor would continue against my will, against my dreams. I would work to survive as my family had done my whole life, and bear the burden of the ones who had abandoned my father to his fate. I saw the challenge ahead, the "knowing," a feeling that it would fall on my shoulders, to prevail long after my parents exhausted themselves pursuing ghostly visions of their dismal future.

It was plainly written on the wall that someone would have to see to the survival of this family, and the burden clearly had my name written all over it. I did question, "Why me?" I wasn't the one who talked them into "wandering, dream-chasing escapades" so late in their life. I wanted no part of their dreams, their shattered dreams.

Regrettably, they foundered, so I began to feel the pressure to fulfill their dreams because I was still within their grip. Therefore, the disparity in my age with the older half-siblings had me in a grid lock, and I saw my life spiraling into more misery and grief because I didn't have a choice.

They all had had their chance. I wanted mine, and my sights were set in the sky. I had looked upon the skies from a sunken ditch for too many years. I envisioned a stairway leading from the deepest irrigation canal, steering me clear of everything known to me in that short period of time. I had come to visualize day after day my dream: to fly a jet plane. Military planes seared the blue heavens leaving a long-lasting "white tail" enticing me to follow it, and disappearing over the horizon. What was at the other end? I wanted to know.

My beliefs would dim those dreams like a greater force was intervening. Did I want to follow a superior force-God? To question: "Is this what you have charged me with? Is this the journey you have paved for me, because it is YOUR will and not mine?" "Is this predestined? Should I stop complaining and accept my fate, because I had no chance to alter events in my life at this point?"

I was averted from taking the direction I wanted to take. I wanted to feel His mighty power. I needed to hear His thundering voice to scold me: "This is what I have chosen for you because this is what I have arranged for you, regardless of your plans for your young life."

Hopelessness came over me – my wings were clipped. I had been sealed with an incredible fate and I felt so much anger and frustration at the unfairness. Any more "pushing His button" would have probably ended with a lightning bolt striking me and that would have been the end of me.

It was my faith in Him that I had come to depend on, but rather what I believed was a spiritual wonder, a caring force I had felt a few years earlier. I felt He should be on my side, not on theirs, and I was butting heads with Him on these points.

Unable to choose for myself, the invisible chains had shackled me to His will. I had been charged with a very heavy mandate, and I understood I must accept it. In essence, I would carry this heavy cross, and the burden to see my parents' end of days. That's a pretty damn heavy charge for a fourteen or fifteen year old to bear. All I wanted was relief from my misery of all those years. I thought I was done! Not quite. I had been chosen.

Shangri-La

"Shangri-La" is the word that describes my father's life quest in the U.S. I researched the origin of this word and why it surfaced in my brain to title this vignette. Shangri-La means a utopia, an imaginary place, a permanently, perfectly happy land isolated from the outside world where aging was almost unheard of and totally mystical in nature. But, it wasn't reality.

I recall a movie I saw at the Julesburg Drive-In sometime in the early sixties. I don't recall the title, but its setting had something to do with a perfect world, trouble free where everything and anything was readily available, without any sacrifice or resistance. Mortality was postponed indefinitely, maybe forever, while the characters vowed to never return to the world they came from. The valley in the kingdom offered them richness beyond their dreams, only available in this kingdom and they would live forever to enjoy this false treasure.

Dad would begin his quest for a better life at the age of fifty years old when he began his trips to Colorado, the Pan Handle and California with a wife, five young adults, and a toddler. Notwithstanding, he envisioned fulfilling his dream of wealth and leisure which resulted in a very high cost to both his health and all the members of our family.

Though he had been in the U.S. for more than ten years, he was already an old man by the time he began migrating. Hard times compounded with hard labor had aged his body beyond his current age. The years working up until then had netted him absolutely nothing in terms of prosperity. He had survived on guts and hope.

He visualized a better life if by, combining his, his children's, and Mom's pay he'd make that dream come true for himself. He needed every possible hand that could walk and earn his/her keep. There would be money in numbers, and so he gambled on his chances in field labor.

He was caught up in the vast illusion thinking that prosperity existed in all these "green valleys." They were really just places to work. His vision of succeeding in field labor was something he believed in, brought on by all the exaggeration of others who fed lies into his head in order to make more money for themselves or to negate the fact that they were working for nothing too.

Aside from our yearly trip to Ovid, every place we went to work suggested by other migrant workers netted him absolutely nothing. Come to think of it, it was the same lying bunch who originally talked him into working the cotton gins in the Pan Handle. We incurred traveling expenses just to get to California, Swink, and the Pan Handle. Those costs offset our actual profits earned while working in Ovid.

Shangri-La was the lifestyle he sought after – the great reward in the distant lands, the Mecca of his visions. In truth, it was a nonexistent place where he had placed his hopes to have his dreams of wealth come true: the place for the dreamer – for my father. This make believe, yet persistent dream kept my father's head in the clouds, thinking there was gold at the end of every place he went to work, drawn to it by all the hoopla and stories of great money made. In the face of defeat he had battled some difficult times unwavering. In the end, he'd succumb to desertion by his own sons.

In the end, there were no rewards, nor gratitude for his efforts.

A Polaroid photo taken in 1967, second to the last year of our trips to Ovid depicts a very tired and worn out man. Included in the photo is Laco Torres, his step-son, the only one left to drive him around. I have my arm around Dad's neck and around Mom, posing in the center of the picture. This is all that was left of his entire "army" of workers. I am looking ahead in my life, with many years left in my existence while he lost out on his. Still, working the fields, his demeanor says it all. In his ten years as a migrant, he had aged three times faster, withering away, a high toll paid for his struggles to survive now more than ever.

The light in his eyes had dimmed. He was done. I knew the time had come to end our traveling. Even though Dad didn't come right out and say it, he didn't have to. It was in his demeanor, on his face, in his deteriorating body. He was tired and worn down, but still a fighter

Dad, Mom and Laco; I think that's me in the middle.

wanting to keep going to see if the magic would yet appear.

Perhaps he sensed an unknown illness gaining on him, and the fact that he had no other support to count on. Everyone else had married and moved on. I was just beginning to make a go of my life at fifteen, and he was ready to let go of his.

The mindless wandering, for next to nothing in pay, there was no stopping him. If there had been twenty four hours of daylight, he'd work through them.

I was powerless to change his mind and get him to stop and yell to him: "Hey, enough! There is no El Dorado out there! It's all lies! Stop dragging us through this hell! Stop dragging me through this misery!" I couldn't bring myself to tell him that because I respected him too much, and I know, in his mind, he was doing the best he could.

He was a gullible person, believing in bogus stories from others who bragged about having earned an extra dollar more.

Believers and my Dad heard these stories from others as to where to find the "pot of gold." The rainbows appearing in the distance could only add to his hope, but in my eyes they represented so much more than what he found, there at the end. He did have his gold: it was his family, and he put them through hell trying to find something better. And they all abandoned him, looking for a better life, one by one.

They wouldn't believe him justifying "Well, this year we didn't make it, but wait till next year." I wasn't fooled by that speech, and neither were my half-brothers. The world I had lived in for those years, living under the conditions we did, just looked all the same, still riddled in poverty. I don't blame them for abandoning him, but it was in the manner they left him: too soon to have given it a chance as a family bound by the similar dreams as his. Maybe, and that's a hard core "maybe," the outcome may have appeased him to settle for more than what he had earned in Texas, by staying put in Ovid- my desire. But now there was no more army of workers to bring in money since we were down to two.

All the while, I struggled to win the right to stay in school. I braced myself for fear of being added to his dwindling supply of workers, but, more importantly, I had come to realize that without an education I would be left with a migrant future or worse. I had to stay focused on my dreams and hope we were nearing the end of this traveling madness.

In the distance, a light waited just for me at the end of the tunnel, so to speak. The light illuminated the path I wanted to follow: to continue my education, be successful, and someday fly over the iridescent-hued horizons I remembered as a child.

The next phase of my life begins . . . . . my most difficult years are still ahead.

Ode to the Migrant Soul

When born, we are sealed with a fate

To be a "soul" whose life we will shape.

Through time we live as though we've known—

Those of us with a "knowing"

We are shackled to the migrants' fields.

Sustained by the very light shone upon us!

The asphalt covered paths appear;

Step by step we mark our traveled paths

In search of the "Shangri-la,"

Of broken promises.

We keep our etched memories,

Enriched by experiences.

There is only one direction in which we look:

To the heavens for the strength to walk

The endless rows and traveled miles of earth.

The cross we bear is that of a sealed fate,

Sent to us, distinguished from the rest.

From light we came, to light we return,

For the Migrant Soul bears a seal of Gold -

One that reigns forever

In the Universe's vault of Love.

– EG

Epilogue

. . . . never can say goodbye

As I wrote these vignettes, I sensed a healing overcome me to finally let go of those years. For decades, I clung on to them not knowing why. They were the most impressionable years of my life, all at the same time, they were heartbreaking, yet euphoric.

Then, the essence of the Blessed Mother Teresa "enlightened" my recollection of this time. Out of pain and suffering, my love and compassion evolved, and I surrendered my heart and soul to her altruistic revelation to write.

I wrote everything I remembered, yet, I am sure there were other stories and experiences that remained entombed in my mind. But, I can tell you that for every moment that I wrote, even as little as a thought, a shred of a memory or a story, my tears splattered on the written words that flowed from the unchartered ravines of my aching soul. By sharing those years with others, it was now 'my time' to forgive, in order to begin the healing process.

To remember the early life I lived is a remarkable God-given gift, and those difficult years determined the person HE willed me to be. I realize, decades later, that my early years were the cobblestone paths intended to scrape my bare feet, and the thorn infested passages that scored me and scarred me - ultimately transforming my soul, like a pearl born from pain.

It is these experiences that drew me to share the importance of the compassion of human spirit with each other. Through sharing, I believe we will find happiness during our earthly stay.

I am blessed, I am thankful, I am content. Thus clearly, I "never can say goodbye" to little Emma from Ovid.

CREDITS

Title Font Design	Emma Isabella Perez
Editor	Mary Ann Escamilla, *Lecturer UTPA Edinburg*
Drawings	Romeo Torres
Back Cover Photo	Abel Riojas Photography
Artwork Design	Ed Rodriguez: *Clear Design Graphics*

For more information about the author, please visit her website:

www.**CountyRd34Publishings**.com

IN HER NEXT BOOK, PATHS OF PEARLS, Emma writes about her life after the migrating years when her parents settle in Edinburg, Texas. From age 15 she struggled to shoulder the financial burdens after her father's death, to support her mother and herself, and fight to pursue her education and happiness. This new lifestyle is so unsettling for her. She draws strength from her past to survive. She shares her reunion, after 50 years, with Ovid, Colorado when she revisited her childhood places and reunited with childhood friends and neighbors.

P.O. Box 3668 • Edinburg, Texas 78540

"Field Mice: Memoirs of a Migrant Child" is a must read. It serves as a reminder of the hellish work that our families of migrant workers of past and present have endured and continue to do so.

It is educational and informative about a way of life of people who help feed the world, but at times themselves go to bed hungry.

"Field Mice" will make you laugh, be sad, but will inspire you to try harder to succeed in life and not to give up on your goals and dreams, to realize the importance of a good education, and to always remember and believe, "QUE SI SE PUEDE!" ("IT CAN BE DONE!")

Finally, like all good things in life, you hate to get to the end of it!
– José María DeLeón Hernández
Little Joe Y La Familia

"The Harvest – October Skies" a vignette from *Field Mice: Memoirs of a Migrant Child* was one of six entries of creative non-fiction published in the *RiverSedge Journal of Art & Literature,* an annual publication by the English Department at the University of Texas-PanAm in Edinburg, Texas. "The Harvest," was one of only 70 works selected from over 600 National as well as International submissions.